TEACHING & LEARNING IN HIGHER EDUCATION

FOR QUENTIN

Who has helped more than he probably realizes with the preparation of this book.

Teaching & Learning in Higher Education

Alice Heim

NFER Publishing Company Ltd.

Published by the NFER Publishing Company Ltd.,
2 Jennings Buildings, Thames Avenue,
Windsor, Berks. SL4 1QS
Registered Office: The Mere, Upton Park, Slough, Berks. SL1 2DQ
First published 1976
© A. W. Heim
ISBN 0 85633 094 9

Printed in Great Britain by
King, Thorne and Stace Ltd., School Road, Hove, Sussex BN3 5JE
Distributed in the USA by Humanities Press Inc.,
Hillary House–Fernhill House, Atlantic Highlands,
New Jersey 07716, USA

Contents

I began writing this book with the technique of lecturing primarily in mind: lecturing in universities, polytechnics and colleges of education, evening lectures for extramural boards and other part-time courses for adults, lectures delivered at specialist conferences and congresses, public lectures on more general themes and luncheon- and tea-club talks. I have had experience in these fields, both as listener and as performer, and the impetus for embarking on a review of lecturing was the realization of how deficient in technique most lecturers are – myself, of course, included. I have observed nodding heads and surreptitious newspaper-reading on many occasions among members of the audience – both when I have been such a member and when I have been giving the lecture. Moreover my own students, whether at university or at college of education, have often complained bitterly to me about the dullness of Green's delivery, the off-putting mannerisms of Black, the inaudibility of Brown and the way in which Grey breathlessly packs into an hour's session far more than his listeners can assimilate and is rarely available to answer queries aroused by his discourses.

I believe that I have learned something from these complaints and from observation of my own audiences – responding sometimes enthusiastically, sometimes apathetically – over the years. I have learned that a monotonous drone can effectively kill excellent material; though I have noted with interest and regret that a charismatic manner will sometimes successfully obscure the fact that the matter is rather weak. Clearly, the ideal is a combination of good material, perceived as relevant, and put over with skill and sparkle. In the early chapters, I attempt to analyse the more frequent defects of lecturers and to suggest ways in which these may be overcome. I assume that most lecturers possess the requisite learning and I therefore concentrate more on manner than on matter. Nevertheless, a few hints are offered with regard to pitching the level of the lecture, setting out the material and excluding, as far as possible, subject matter which is readily available in books and journals.

Since the first five chapters concern lecturing, it is evident that I believe this system of teaching to be potentially valuable and also that I think that (after some six centuries) it is here to stay. In the course of writing, however, I became more deeply involved in examining other

techniques of teaching and learning in higher education and realized that
other methods, supplementary to the lecture method, also merit
discussion.

Thus, Chapters VI to VIII deal with the arts/science comparison, the
tutorial and the compiling of booklists and handouts. Chapters IX to XI
concern research – at every level; and chapter XII discusses the seminar
as a means of instruction. These middle chapters are perhaps more concerned with specifically *university* teaching than are the earlier ones,
though much that is said may apply in colleges of education and in
polytechnics.

Student assessment and teacher assessment are dealt with in Chapters
XIII and XIV, these being considered pertinent to all fields of higher
education, including sixth forms. The last three chapters examine the
rationale of education and discuss the paradoxical nature of freedom
of speech among teachers and taught.

The book abounds in generalizations, yet I am aware that the approach
to teaching and learning varies with the discipline and with the individual. The titles of Chapters II and III highlight my dilemma. When
pontificating about teaching, one is apt either to state the obvious or to
assert one's own personal, controversial viewpoint. Being a psychologist, this is a dilemma with which I am familiar – and familiarity has
perhaps here bred resignation. It is *not* unnecessary, however, to state
'the obvious' in teaching, since some teachers fail to fulfil the basic
conditions for communication. Nor is the assertion of a controversial
statement invariably useless: it may give grounds for thought. This is
the main aim of the book.

ACKNOWLEDGEMENTS AND DISCLAIMERS

Warm thanks are due to Mrs Sheila Unwin, Mr Eric Southall and Dr Peter Stone for their kindness in reading the typescript and helping, in many places, to clarify the English and the ideas. I am most grateful, too, to Mr Michael Abercrombie and the late Mr John Scott for their generous and expert assistance in providing me with pure → applied and applied → pure examples for my ninth chapter; and to Dr Jane Abercrombie for her help with the chapter on the Seminar. Dr Timothy Smiley expressed kind interest, and offered me useful suggestions in the early stages of the book. Dr Gyorgy Erdos was very helpful on the question of the controversy on educational aims and also in drawing my attention to the bibliogaphy on *University Teaching* compiled by the Library Resources Section of the University of Newcastle-on-Tyne.

I give thanks also to Mrs Laurie Turner for her impeccable typing and – at times, positively psychic – deciphering of my handwriting. Acknowledgements are due also to *Punch* for permission to use a cartoon of theirs on the cover of this book. I am very grateful to the Medical Research Council for their encouragement and financial support over the years.

I should like to express gratitude too to the many teachers and students who have, albeit often unwittingly, provided raw material for this book. All the anecdotes are founded on fact but all the colour-names are fictitious. Where real names are used, they can be recognized by the fact that they are never, it so happens, the name of a colour and – to make assurance double sure – they are usually preceded by a first name or an initial.

On the question of names, I should like to make one last disclaimer. A publisher's reader made the comment that I appear in this book to be concerned wholly with men, as opposed to women. At first I found this pronouncement astounding (not unnaturally, I have them both equally in mind). It then occurred to me that he – or, possibly she – was unfamiliar with the use of the male pronoun to signify people generally, in the same way as 'mankind' denotes women as well as men. Moreover, I later realized that he might always imagine a male figure, when reading of, for instance, Dr Sable or Professor Argent. I therefore embrace this opportunity of disclaiming any tendency towards male chauvinism, piggish or otherwise; and I have carefully inserted the phrase 'or her' on the first occasion in which it seems appropriate – namely, line one of chapter one – in the hope that the reader will thereafter indulge either in hermaphroditic imagery or picture a member of each sex – not perhaps in strict turn, but in roughly the ratio which at present obtains in British institutions of higher learning.

'A powerful idea communicates some of its strength to him who challenges it.'   Marcel PROUST.

'Find more pleasure in intellectual dissent than in passive agreement, for, if you value intelligence as you should, the former implies a deeper agreement than the latter.'   Bertrand RUSSELL.

'The end of education is to render the individual, as much as possible, an instrument of happiness, first to himself and next to others.'   James MILL, father of John Stuart MILL.

'There are not two sciences. There is only science and the application of science and these two activities are linked as the fruit is to the tree.' Louis PASTEUR.

'Education is discipline for the adventure of life; research is intellectual adventure; and the universities should be homes of adventure shared in common by young and old.'   A. N. WHITEHEAD.

Chapter 1

The aims of lecturing: some criticisms answered

'One of the great objects of education is to accustom a young man *gradually* to become his own master'.

Sydney SMITH

'I am inclined to think that Ministers of Government require almost as much education in their trade as shoe-makers or tallow-chandlers'. Anthony TROLLOPE

A lecturer asked what are his (or her) aims in giving a course of lectures is apt to reply – with an attempt at humour, seen all too seldom by his students – that he does it to earn his salary: probably true and certainly not very funny. If pushed, however, he may say something like 'I aim to inculcate knowledge in the young' or 'It's still regarded as one of the best ways of teaching facts'. Rarely will he say: 'to stimulate interest' or 'to provoke discussion'; and still more rarely will he attain these objectives.

The purpose of the first chapters of this book is to plead that these should be the major aims of the lecturer and to suggest means of achieving them. There are enough textbooks and journals from which the student may acquire the relevant facts and theories – if he is reading science; and may acquaint himself with fine language and literature – if he is reading arts. The lecturer should not attempt to fulfil the same functions as books. All students can read, in theory, and any who do not enjoy doing so should probably not be students at all. Moreover they can read relaxedly, at their own pace, in their own chosen surroundings (feet on table, in silent concentration or tap-tapping to the accompaniment of powerful pop); they can take their reading 'massed' or 'spaced' as the psychologists put it; they can change their book, discard it or even re-read it, if they feel so disposed.

The lecture does not possess these advantages of the book or the journal – save that it too can be 'discarded', in the sense that the student can walk out or go to sleep, the latter course evidently being regarded as the more courteous of the two. But the lecture does have, or should have, the advantages of being 'live'. These include spontaneity, novelty, flexibility and there is of course always the chance of something going wrong! This is a wonderful recipe for enlivening the proceedings – if, indeed, they need enlivening. One of the objects of this book is to suggest methods of imparting animated enjoyment, and even sometimes amusement, to lectures. Many lecturers behave as though gaiety is incompatible with enlightenment. It is my belief that the greater the enjoyment – and the participation – in a lecture, the greater the benefit to the student. In such relaxed, cheerful circumstances, he will not *be indoctrinated:* this would be lamentable (although some lecturers unwittingly aim at this). It would ensure a static condition of knowledge and thought, devoutly to be shunned.

It is not fortuitous that the phrase 'he read me a lecture on . . .' (mark the word 'read') is usually equated with the phrase 'he preached me a sermon on . . .'. Indeed, the relevant section in Roget's *Thesaurus* ('lecture: teach') goes: 'read – give a lesson, – lecture, – sermon, – discourse; hold forth, preach; sermon-, moral-ize; point a moral.'

The view taken in this book is that the lecturer should aim at communication with his students and that communication is essentially a two-way process. This can be observed in the commercial theatre, during a successful performance. Even in productions which do not solicit participation, the audience laughs, weeps, holds its breath or bursts into spontaneous applause. In less successful performances, the spectators creakingly shift position, blow their noses and crackle sweet-papers. The player responds sensitively to the reactions of his listeners. The lecturer should do no less.

It is fully realized that lecturing is not the be-all and end-all of teaching in universities and other institutions of higher learning. Many serious students (and the breed is not extinct) systematically eschew lectures, whilst others avoid them less systematically, the occasional attendance of the latter students being motivated by a speaker whom they find exceptionally stimulating or by a topic which particularly interests them.

Such students may prefer the relative independence of the one-to-one tutorial, the small seminar, the individual research project, the 'practical' in natural sciences, the writing of essays and informal discussion with their peers. All these make – or ought to make – an important contribution to post-school learning; and they are considered in later chapters. For many students these complement, rather than supplement, attendance at lectures. But the lecture remains for most university teachers, and for many students, the most illuminating entrance to the edifice of higher education.

For this reason, roughly the first third of this book is concerned with lecturing. The later part deals with other methods of teaching and also with techniques of appraisal – both of teachers and students. These include questionnaires, continuous assessment, multiple-choice items and examinations – both traditional and experimental. Finally, some answers are offered to the questions, 'why assess ?' and 'what are the aims of higher education ?'

The suggestion that effective lecturing can to some extent be taught, usually evokes one of two reactions. Either the would-be instructor is told that if potential lecturers were actually taught their trade, then everybody 'would lecture in the same way' – a disastrous state of affairs. Or he is informed that some of his suggestions are so obvious that they are unnecessary and the rest are so controversial that they are useless! The implication of these sceptics is that the good lecturer, like the good cook, is born and not made and that, in any case, experience will do the trick.

Let us consider in turn these various assertions. Lecturing is probably the only professional skill which is *not* taught – and which it is taken for granted does not need to be learned. Most lecturers have an excellent working knowledge of their subject-matter but this does not imply an ability for communicating it. If an author fails to arouse interest and enjoyment in his book, he reaps his own bitter fruits: the book sells poorly, and his royalties and reputation remain meagre. But if a lecturer, once appointed, fails to stimulate interest in his students, he may continue relentlessly to give his courses – sometimes unchanged over the years.

School teachers are given instruction and experience in teaching; and if they fail in this part of their course, they fail to qualify, no matter how brilliantly they may have done in other respects. Yet they do not all teach 'in the same way'. Even those who have been to the same College of Education and been trained to teach the same subjects, develop their own individual style. This objection – about all trained lecturers behaving identically – is on a par with a criticism which used to be made by opponents of intelligence testing as an aid to university student selection: that it would not do to have all the students indistinguishable from one another! Anyone who has researched or taught in a university department – where the majority of the staff are graduates with high and narrow-ranging IQs – would emphatically deny similarity of attitudes, manners, temperament or character among these members of staff.

There is thus no danger of all lecturers giving their courses 'in the same way' – which would indeed be a disaster – even if they all took some instruction in lecturing. This expressed fear is merely an unsuccessful rationalization on the part of opponents of the idea of teaching lecturers to do their job. The only feature they are likely to share is lack of the common faults of the inadequate lecturer. These are, typically, inaudibility in the back rows (which are apt to be far more popular with students than are the front rows); unintelligibility (owing to the confusion, frequent among lecturers, of obscurity of presentation with profundity of thought); and the compulsion to cram into an hour, $1\frac{1}{4}$ hour's worth of information.

These three typical faults are said to be 'obvious' mistakes to avoid. It is, of course, obvious that students should be able to hear and to understand what is said and also that they should not get an impression of flurried haste from their lecturer. On the other hand, this is more easily said than done. The above phenomena occur so frequently and so continuously in the lecture hall that a few hints on their avoidance may be desirable. These are given in Chapter II.

How about the other criticism? – that any recommendations about good lecturing which are not obvious will be highly controversial. This should be taken more seriously. It is true that many suggestions made in this book are indeed debatable: for instance that the lecturer should seek primarily to stimulate rather than inform; that he should foster a light-hearted atmosphere; and that he should virtually substitute a seminar for a monologue.

Some lecturers will certainly disagree with such ideas. Some may think well of them but find them difficult if not impossible to implement. My reasons for including such controversial issues are two. First, I believe, as stated above, that it is both desirable and inevitable that lecturers should differ in manner and in technique. I hope there will be something for everyone in the pages which follow, but it is not anticipated that everybody will agree on all points. This leads to my second reason: I hope to stimulate and to challenge in this book, just as I suggest one should do when lecturing. It is far easier to arouse interest and to stimulate discussion if one explores the forests of controversy than if one strides the highway of certitude.

The two next points for discussion may be considered together. These concern the view that the good lecturer is born and not made and that he can acquire all the expertise he needs through experience. It is clear that some have more natural talent for lecturing than others. This is true of car-driving, painting, child-rearing, lip-reading, eating with chopsticks and most other skills. Though it is perhaps worth mentioning in passing that, however prolonged their training, some could never learn to pilot an aircraft and some could never master violin-playing. We should perhaps recall, however, the important part played by 'compensation' in highly motivated individuals: the great orator, Demosthenes, is well-known (or at least widely believed) to have had a stutter and the much admired Dame Peggy Ashcroft does have a lisp.

Undoubtedly, people lacking the natural gifts of the lecturer – a carrying voice, verbal fluency, clear enunciation, easy breath control, genuine or apparent self possession – can and do acquire proficiency in lecturing. But it seems hard on their students that they should be expected to gain their proficiency by painful experience alone, i.e. at the expense of numerous batches of bored or frustrated listeners. Experience certainly helps; it is often the only way in which to gain the necessary confidence; but there is no reason why the experience of lecturing should not be supplemented, concurrently or in advance, by relevant instruction.

Chapter II

'Obvious, hence unnecessary'

'Will everybody at the back who can't hear me please
raise their hands!' Traditional

In this chapter we shall examine some of the more obvious requisites
of lecturing – those attributes which are necessary, though far from
sufficient, to ensure understanding on the part of the listener. To
effect understanding is not, of course, the same thing as to arouse
interest though some degree of understanding is probably essential to
interest. The two are not wholly separable; nor, indeed, are most of the
features of lecturing discussed here and later. But those suggestions
offered, with interest and stimulation more specifically in mind, are
inevitably more controversial and these therefore appear in later
chapters.

The 'obvious' features fall under eight headings: audibility, unavailability of the material elsewhere, intelligibility, order of subject-
matter, visibility, pitching of level of difficulty, rate of presentation
and the amount of material to be included. All these are dealt with in the
present chapter.

The present fashion of talking among most young people, including
students, is a throw-away style of speech. It arose, presumably, as a
reaction against the 'public school accent' and the 'BBC voice' and
it is reflected in the recent move of Broadcasting House to incorporate
different sorts of accents and voices among its newscasters and givers
of talks. The recognition and welcoming of variety – and, hence, the
discouragement of affectation and adoption of a 'Haw-Haw' tone of
voice – is surely an excellent thing. But it is unfortunate that the current
cult should incline also towards a mumbling, stumbling delivery,
derived from reluctance to open one's mouth, to move one's lips and to

raise one's voice. There is also a tendency to use the phrases 'you know', 'sort of' and 'all right ?' in place of more conventional punctuation. This is particularly hard on the partially deaf and the not-so-young, of whom there are usually a few in every lecture.

Many lecturers, of all ages, speak faintly or unclearly. In some, this is due to shyness and embarrassment, natural enough when embarking on one's first lectures, and curable – if the lecturer is convinced of its importance – by training, auditory aids and experience. Such aids will also help the novice who, without necessarily being self-conscious, happens to have a naturally weak or dry voice. He can learn to make the most of it, to 'project' it, even to ensure if necessary that a microphone will be available.

More difficult to train are those whose vocal deficiency is due to an unwitting arrogance: an unconscious belief that if they speak sufficiently softly, everyone will strain to hear and silence will reign in the lecture hall. This does not work if the hall is large and without microphone, nor if the lecture material is dull.

The requisite volume and clarity will vary with the size and the acoustic properties of the hall. These must be gauged on entering it; in some cases, it may be wise to try out an unfamiliar venue beforehand – bearing in mind that the acoustics are always worse when the hall is empty. But vocal skills may need to be developed and this is probably best achieved by means of recording and playing back, as is done in language laboratories. A few general guidelines, however, may be offered.

There is a tendency when speaking English to drop the voice, in pitch and in volume, at the end of a sentence. This can be frustrating for the listener, especially when the most significant words come at the end of a sentence. The voice should therefore be 'kept up' here; and it should be raised also for the most vital words, wherever they occur. It is not infrequent for the listener to hear everything in a sentence *except* the crucial word or phrase and, in these circumstances, there is not always sufficient redundancy to infer what the sentence was actually about.

Related to this is the question of the emphasis in a sentence. When reading aloud, it is astonishingly easy to stress an inappropriate word, thus subtly altering the meaning of the passage and adding to the difficulties of the listener. One is especially liable to mis-emphasize when nervous or tired or when, for a moment, one's attention wanders. For this reason it may be desirable – if *reading* one's lecture – to underline the word or words in each sentence which need stressing. The merits and demerits of reading as opposed to speaking, from or without notes, are discussed in Chapter IV.

Apart from keeping up the voice at the end of a sentence and emphasizing crucial words, there is the question of variety. A speaker who varies his pace and intonation is easier on the ear than is one who plods on to the end in the same colourless (or raucous) tone. Even if his subject matter is interesting, he is likely to acquire the reputation of being a dull lecturer. 'He is better to read than hear,' say his students – and 'it's all in his books anyway!'

This leads to the second point. University teachers should not simply deliver, as lectures, unchanged material which they have published in book form. In view of the frequency with which lecturers err in this respect, this stricture might be considered controversial. But it is surely clear that students should not be expected to sit and listen to subject matter identical with what is already published. As pointed out earlier, a book can be read both faster and in a more leisurely way than a lecture can be absorbed. Once his book is published, the author may – if he still wishes to use it as a basis for a lecture course – comment, elaborate, annotate, criticize, question, promote discussion, but not (as lecturers both eminent and lowly have been known to do) assiduously read out every paragraph, several times, complete with the familiar examples and jokes. The main advantage of lecturing is, or should be, that it is live, flexible, and to some extent unpredictable.

Apart from the tedium of listening word-for-word to what has already been read, it should be recognized that the written word and the spoken word are two very different media. Books are written to be seen and not heard; conversely, lectures should be composed to be heard and not seen. Thus the manner should be changed as well as the matter, if the lectures are to be a success. The spoken word is less formal, less heavy, more colloquial; the sentences should be shorter; the occasional split infinitive and prepositional ending do not shock; 'have not frequently been conducted' becomes 'haven't often been done'. The very vocabulary is different, as has been demonstrated by laborious word-counts.

These injunctions are linked with the question of intelligibility. The reader of a book can re-read the last couple of pages if he has not taken them in, but the listener to a lecture can do no such thing. Nor is it desirable, in my view, for the speaker to repeat every sentence two or three times to enable the slower student to keep up. Many members of his audience may find this insulting or, worse, boring. It should be possible to organize a lecture so that the main points can be understood, or at least noted, at first hearing. Ideally the listener can take in what he hears, at the same time that he makes the occasional note. This is one of the skills which the student has to acquire, but the lecturer should try to aid him in so doing.

Complete intelligibility cannot, in fact, always be achieved. Certain concepts are unfamiliar, technical terms may have to be introduced, some ideas and relationships are intrinsically difficult to grasp. The extent of these problems varies with the topic being taught – but varies at least as much with the teacher's clarity of mind and the amount of trouble he is prepared to take in the cause of lucidity. I have talked with many lecturers whose students tell me that they find their courses incomprehensible. One student said to me, 'I'm sure only about 5 per cent of the class can understand Mr White. I certainly can't.' When I passed on this comment, White replied complacently, 'Frankly, Alice, I'm only interested in the top 5 per cent.' He seemed totally unaware of the fact that members of this particular minority group could probably manage quite well on their own.

The case of Dr Rose was rather different. When I told him of the several complaints of obscurity I had received from students attending his lectures he replied, with apparent seriousness, that if any one of his lectures was not found baffling, he considered it a failure. He evidently belonged to the school of thought which equates incomprehensibility with wisdom. He has long since retired but many lecturers (and writers) after him adopt the same perverse attitude.

The case of Dr Indigo is different again. On being told by his students that they could not understand his last lecture, he gave the same lecture again, unchanged, at the subsequent session. On being informed that the difficulties had scarcely diminished, he obligingly delivered the identical lecture for the third time – 'and this time', confessed the lecturer, 'even *I* understood it!' Indigo showed a commendable humility and spirit of co-operation. But I still think that he might have done better to understand his own material from the beginning sufficiently well to be able to communicate it on the first occasion. It is often only when trying to teach something – or even to submit it for discussion – that one realizes the extent of one's own confusion.

Intelligibility is closely linked with order of presentation in lecturing – indeed, also in writing. The re-ordering of several sections or the reversing of first and second halves will occasionally produce a sudden vivid clarity, where all had been misty chaos. Once this is realized in a particular instance one wonders how the original order could ever have been contemplated. If this is true of oneself as speaker, what an immensely bigger role must it play for a captive audience, who does not know what is coming and may be uncertain as to what has gone before!

> ' "Knockespotch was a little obscure, sometimes, wasn't he ?" "He was", Mr. Scogan replied, "and with intention. It made him seem even profounder than he actually was".'
>
> Aldous HUXLEY

I think there are few guidelines here, apart from the recommendation to construct one's lecture notes in an adaptable, loose-leaf form to begin with and to bear in mind that the most logical order for the material is not necessarily the best order for the listener. Introductions, for instance, are often more appreciated, paradoxically, at the end than at the beginning of a lecture course. The old saw, 'Tell them what you're going to say; then say it; and then tell them what you've said', is not bad advice – providing that the same form of words is never used more than once.

This latter counsel is strangely important and is useful in many fields, including interviewing, writing, speech-making and ordinary conversation. There are two reasons why, if the lecturer is going to repeat himself, he should not do so word-for-word. His brighter students will probably notice the phenomonon and may 'switch off'. His slower students who may have failed to take in the point on first hearing are far more likely to assimilate it on second hearing, if it is differently expressed. The original failure to communicate may be due to students' unfamiliarity with the concepts but it may equally well be due to an infelicitous mode of expression – in which case a change will probably be for the better.

In view of what I have said about designing lectures to be heard and not seen, it may seem curious to include 'visibility' in a list of lecturing desiderata. Visual aids, however, are increasingly employed and the simple blackboard has of course been used by teachers from time immemorial. School teachers are instructed and practised in writing large and clear on the board; they learn to refrain from obtruding their body between their writing (or drawing) and their audience; and to check that every member of the class can get the message without strain. Moreover, they are instructed to put up on the board proper names and unfamiliar words, in order that their pupils may add the visual to the auditory clues and may acquire the correct spelling.

These precepts are evidently thought to be unnecessary for university students; or perhaps, on the contrary, their value is deemed so obvious that lecturers are expected to follow them implicitly. Both viewpoints are, I think, mistaken. Students of every level need, and like, *to see* the novel word or symbol. And lecturers, like other teachers, need to learn when it is essential to use the blackboard and how to render their efforts legible.

The same counsel applies when an epidiascope or an overhead projector is used to present data. These tend to be in the form of tables, formulae, graphs, maps or pictures. It is quite frequent for lecturers at conferences and meetings, as in university courses, to put up carefully prepared slides or transparencies which cannot be seen adequately by people at the back. Furthermore, whether clear or indistinct, they sometimes contain an abundance of information, that cannot be assimilated during a rapid viewing – and the time allowed is often woefully brief. During a longer presentation, it is sometimes impossible to interpret the figures and to take in at the same time what the lecturer is saying. Evidently the best way to use visual aids is something that has to be learned and, interestingly, it is *not* learned through experience of having been at the receiving end.

One further point about visual material: some lecturers, aware of the problems of legibility and the varying time required for individuals to digest the information projected on a screen, prepare duplicated sheets and hand them round for inspection during the lecture. Given this strategy, it is possible to offer a few guidelines.

If there are, say, three sheets of data these should be appropriately labelled and stapled together; and there should be enough copies for every student to have, and to retain, the sheets. Do not expect to get them back, uncreased and free from finger marks, ready for next year's class! Do not expect the students to know by some telepathic process which datum is being referred to: give its number and heading and, if necessary, its position on the page. Do not distribute among, say, fifty students a dozen sets to pass round as you speak: their attention will be divided between watching the progress of the sets and listening to the lecture. Above all, do not expect the students to absorb the information on the sheets and, simultaneously, to register what the lecturer is saying when these two do not coincide.

The next three points are particularly closely related. They concern pitching the level of difficulty, rate of delivery and amount of material to include. Most school teachers are acutely aware of the difference between teaching, for instance, the lower fourth and the upper fifth. They know that the latter will tend to be better listeners with a longer span of concentration, that more members of the class will find the subject matter intrinsically interesting and that they can understand more complex ideas and follow more challenging lines of thought. This is partly due to the fact that the fifth formers know more of the relevant background and partly to their greater age. The teacher there-fore pitches the level of difficulty higher for the older pupils, whatever topic he may be dealing with. He usually aims for the middle ranges of whichever class hoping, in this way, not to antagonize the high-flyers because the lesson is too simple for them and, equally, not to frighten the slower pupils who easily feel out of their depth.

This pitching of level is in itself highly skilled and of course it becomes harder as the range of ability in the class widens. (Those who enthusiastically crusade, against streaming and in favour of mixed ability classes in school, might sometimes ponder this point. Greater problems for the teacher create greater problems – both intellectual and disciplinary – for the taught.) Schoolmasters and mistresses are instructed in the art of appropriate pitching and this instruction is strongly reinforced by their experience in the teaching profession. They are constantly receiving immediate 'feedback'.

Since most university teachers are expected to lecture by the light of nature, they receive neither the instruction nor, very often, the necessary feedback. There are two points to consider here: first, the general level of the students attending the lecture course, e.g. first year general or third year specialists; and, secondly, the question of level *within* the group, e.g. the potential firsts, the probable thirds or the majority who fall between these two extremes.

Both these points demand thought. Lecturers are sometimes so obsessed by their subject matter that they fail to ask themselves how their talks will come over, and how extended or limited is the intellectual background of their listeners. I heard not long ago a public lecture by a world authority on a topic on the borders of economics and anthrop-ology; the audience was exceedingly mixed, containing academics of all ages and all disciplines. Yet every listener with whom I later discussed the lecture was agreed that, save for his concluding three sentences, the speaker had not stimulated their interest nor told them anything of which they had previously been unaware.

Probably in this instance the lecturer had deliberately pitched his talk low, confining himself to generalities in view of the mixed composition of his audience. He had, however, failed to take into account what his listeners had in common, namely, wide general knowledge and keen interest in current affairs. Moreover, generalities without concrete examples tend to be platitudinous. Finally, he gained no feedback since public lectures are not followed by public discussion. Thus one of the most fruitful methods of checking one's lecturing manner and matter was closed to him and he is likely to continue to give public lectures of a similar kind.

Assuming, however, that the lecturer is well aware of the general nature and level of his audience, he still has to decide where – within that level – he will pitch his talk. I believe that to aim it at the high-flyers, the 'top 5 per cent' is basically self-indulgent: it constitutes rather an extension of his own research than a determined effort to communicate. The exceptionally able student tends to thrive, with or without lectures. However, to aim at the other extreme is, in my view, also mistaken.

Most groups of students conform to the 'normal distribution', that is, the majority of them are – almost by definition – average for the student population in ability, interest, background knowledge and willingness to work. Experienced and effective lecturers often state that they aim at the second classes and this should surely be the aim of most university teachers. The second classes usually constitute a majority and they also form a bridge between the brilliant and the relatively obtuse. If one pitches one's lecture for the average, one is unlikely to offend any subgroup, provided that one fulfils one's aim. This, however, is at least as difficult as it is to pitch successfully at baseball. Both require practice and feedback: the latter is discussed in chapter XIII. It suffices here to point out that the lecturer should appreciate the problems of pitching as worthy of consideration and that he should realize, having decided on the required 'level', that further thought is needed if he is to succeed in his choice. Establishing the level and the range of his audience is part of his task in preparing lectures.

Rate of presentation and amount of material to include can be discussed together. The lecturing novice is usually haunted by the spectre of running out of material. He pictures himself, horrified, with 20 minutes to spare at the end of the session, having come to the end of his notes. The inexperienced lecturer is, typically, very conscientious: he would not dream of leaving his class early. He tends also to be scared of his students and it does not therefore strike him as practicable to have a free-for-all in the event of his finishing before time.

For these reasons, and also because experience is needed to time a talk for exactly 50 or 55 minutes, the novice tends to prepare too much material for his first lectures. Indeed, he may well try to cram too much into his whole course. This failing is in fact not confined to novices. The error of including too much, of not rehearsing it and of insisting on making the hapless audience sit through to the end, refusing to delete a single pearl despite the marching of time, is all too common in the after-dinner speaker, the school speech-day guest-of-honour, the reader of papers at conferences and the university lecturer. Where a strong chairman presides, willing to play his part, the restless tedium may be avoided. But there is, of course, no chairman in university lectures and if the lecturer sees fit to continue right up to the end of the hour, or beyond it, there is usually no stopping him. Even if his successor in the lecture hall bangs on the door or expostulates at 11.5, the incumbent is likely to plead, 'just three more minutes'!

This behaviour is based on several misconceptions, of which the first is the evident belief that students can take in what is being said while they are collecting their books, climbing over desks or worrying about arriving late at their next lecture or their coffee appointment. Secondly, an hour's lecture (i.e. 50 minutes' worth, since lectures last traditionally from, for instance, 10.5 to 10.55) is about the longest period of sustained concentration of which most people are capable. Moreover, this is the length which the students are *expecting* and resentment tends to build up if they are detained for longer. It is only the exceptionally gifted lecturer who can hold their interest for a longer period – and he has probably said, vividly and concisely, all that he has to say in 45 or 50 minutes.

Thirdly, as the clock hands approach 10.55, the lecturer becomes flurried. He says to himself that he must at all costs get to the end of the section and, with this end in view, his delivery suffers. He hurries; he ineffectually apologizes; he forgets to keep his voice up; above all, he does not realize that he has lost whatever rapport he had attained with his students.

It is true that the lecturer can transgress in the other direction. If his lecture notes are too sparse, the material may not last for 50 minutes. This need hold no terror for the competent lecturer who will probably be relaxed enough to embroider around a theme or he may solicit questions and comments from his audience. The latter procedure is highly desirable but the new young lecturer may as yet lack the necessary confidence. In that event his best tactics are to rehearse his lecture in advance, in order to establish how long it lasts, and to take into the lecture hall more material than he thinks he will need for one lecture.

The guidelines concerning rate of presentation and amount of material to include are now emerging. The first is on no account to lecture for longer than 50–55 minutes, even if this entails omitting one or two favourite points. These will be better dealt with at the beginning of the subsequent lecture, when the speaker and his audience are fresh. Secondly, a certain amount of overlap in subject matter between the end of one lecture and the start of the next is advisable, provided that the same form of words is not repeated. This is desirable because the very beginning and the very end of a lecture are not ideal times for communication: even in a strictly 50 minute talk, the beginning and the end are liable to certain noises and disturbances as people walk along the corridors, latecomers arrive and the blackboard is found to be full of hieroglyphics left by the previous lecturer.

Thirdly, the lecturer should speak more slowly than one does in normal conversation. His speed should suit those of his listeners who hear least well and understand most slowly. Some of his students will probably prefer to listen only, but in every audience are found a few inveterate note-takers who feel cheated if they cannot take down most of what is said.

Finally, it is worth remembering that the proportion absorbed by students generally is inversely related to the number of points made in a lecture. Only when one has had experience in essay-reading and examination-marking does one realize the appalling facility with which students get hold of the wrong end of the stick. This sometimes results from their reading, but more often from their sitting in lecture halls. Thus the amount of material to incorporate should usually be a compromise between the wealth of facts or opinions which the lecturer would like to include and the half-dozen major points which must at all costs be made. In the last resort, the decision rests of course with the individual lecturer and his particular style. Providing he is aware that more words-per-minute does not imply more learning on the part of his students, the selection and density of information purveyed should rest comfortably with him.

Chapter III

'*Controversial, hence useless*'

I hear and I forget
I see and I remember
I do and I understand
                              Chinese proverb

My most controversial suggestion about lecturing is that the formal university lecture should be superseded by discussion or seminar-type teaching. A frequent response to this recommendation from fellow lecturers is that this is all very well for small classes, 'for those who like that sort of thing', but that it is plainly impossible for large classes of 50–100 or more: the practical problems of managing discussions in a large, echoing lecture hall, the reticence of students, the unavailability to them of the microphone, the difficulties of covering the syllabus and of maintaining order – these and other plausible obstacles are put forward by those who prefer the authority and prestige conveyed by an uninterrupted monologue.

Students, on the other hand, welcome the chance of gaining clarification on some point as it occurs, of commenting on or requesting elaboration on some aspect of particular interest and of expressing disagreement or putting another viewpoint if they have already given some thought to the topic. It can be irritating to have to wait to ask a pertinent question – which unanswered may impair understanding of the rest of the lecture – particularly if the student rightly suspects that there may not be time to pose the question at the end of the session.

I am not proposing that the lecturer should simply announce his topic for the hour and thenceforward, completely dispensing with lecture notes, rely on the whims of his students. My suggestion is that he should have sufficient notes to last to the end of the session in the event of no general discussion being aroused, and that he should make it clear from the beginning that he welcomes relevant contributions. He should, in fact, judge his lecture unsuccessful if he fails to provoke any overt reactions from his audience.

Listening, hearing and even note-taking are more passive forms of behaviour than are questioning, commenting and arguing. The more active the student, the more involved he becomes with his subject matter and with his fellow students. Those of his peers who do not speak will gain more from the lively give-and-take of discussion, the varied personalities and points of view, than they will from a monologue, however well structured. If one student raises a particular question, the odds are that some others share the same doubt. Indeed, this is usually clear from the several eagerly nodding heads which often accompany a question.

Students in general like this method. They greatly prefer it to the formal lecture and they prefer it, too, to the system adopted by some lecturers, of reserving a few minutes at the end for discussion (and many university teachers do not even make this concession). Those lecturers who have tried the participation technique and condemn it, generally do so on several grounds. They claim that many of the points raised are trivial or, on the other hand, that they were proposing to deal with just those points more conveniently, later in the session. They maintain that it is impossible to cover the syllabus or, indeed, to plan the course, if they do not know how much time to allow for lecturing and how much for dealing with interruptions – for this is how they regard the students' comments.

Trivial points may arise from one of two causes. They tend to emanate either from the rare student who, conceited and self-opinionated, cannot let pass an opportunity for inflicting on others the sound of his own voice. He can generally be recognized by his persistence and insensibility and by the fact that his questions are thinly disguised statements of his own dogmatic opinion.

Such an assertive individual often asks questions in the belief that he knows the answer, and he may need to be discouraged by the lecturer – this to be done on an intellectual rather than an emotional level – but such action can usually be safely left to the other students. They recognize the pretentious trouble-maker at least as quickly as does the teacher and they have no desire to let such time-wasters monopolize the time of the class.

Trivia may, however, come from a worried, diffident student who has genuine difficulty in keeping up, and in distinguishing the wood from the trees. It is important not to wound the latter by demonstrating in one's reply the paucity of his contribution or the fact that the matter has already been dealt with. If a satisfactory public response prove impossible, the best plan is probably to offer to deal with the point personally, at the end of the session – and, of course, to do so.

Now to those contributions, far more frequent, which merit public discussion. The plea that the lecturer was shortly to deal with the particular point raised, needs careful examination. It is doubtless often true that a student anticipates a point which had duly been entered in the teacher's notes and which he was looking forward to making in his own time. But if a student raises the issue now, *now* is very likely the time to deal with it from the point of view of the student.

I have suggested above that there is rarely a single best order of presentation. All the relevant points should be included, but the teacher should not be perturbed if they are not invariably introduced in the intended order or if some of them get postponed to a subsequent session, or even omitted from the course. He should be prepared to be flexible, and to realize that his lectures are *for the benefit of the students*. Their purpose is not to enable him to get his own ideas straight: this should be achieved before he embarks on his lecture course, although admission of occasional uncertainty or ignorance is sometimes desirable. It can prove stimulating to the students and it tends to renew their faith in the lecturer.

Again, preparing a lecture course should not be identified with writing a book. The lecture notes, plus contributions from students, may prove a useful basis for eventual publication but, as indicated above, this is not a case where two birds can be killed with one stone (whether thrown forwards or backwards). The attempt to do so will merely result in two sadly maimed avians. A textbook should be comprehensive within its field and, once published, its form is of course strictly determined and unalterable. A lecture course, on the other hand, need not be comprehensive – since it is supplemented by reading and tutorials* – and it should not be so rigid that students cannot be allowed a say. They will lose more than they gain if the lecturer adheres obdurately to his preconceived ideas and order of presentation.

It is naturally easier to conduct seminar type lectures with a select

---

*'Tutorial' at Oxford = 'supervision' at Cambridge. Other universities no doubt have their own names for the staff–student personal discussions – which are considered in chapter VII.

group, in a small room, than it is with, say, 150 students in a necessarily large lecture hall. The latter is feasible, however, if the lecturer is persuaded of its value. He may need to pause, or actively to solicit comments, during his first session, but once the students are convinced of his goodwill and his interest in what they have to say, they will usually co-operate with enthusiasm. The introverts may hold back but their more fluent, outgoing peers will speak up, and speak on their behalf. Students, like other animate beings, *behave in accordance with the way they are treated*. If they are treated as sponges, capable merely of instant absorption and subsequent regurgitation, this is how most of them will behave. But if they are expected to take an active, critical, constructive part in their course, they will in general do so – with benefit both to themselves and their teacher.

If the lecturer feels that his subject matter or the conditions in which he is teaching, preclude the give-and-take of free discussion while he is talking, then he would be well advised to set aside 10–15 minutes at the end of the session, to be devoted to questions and comments. He should inform his listeners of his plan, at the beginning of the first few sessions (until the students are used to the idea) and he should on no account cut short the time for discussion, however much he may be tempted to do so by having failed to cover all the points he considers essential. I see this scheme as a compromise between the (ideal) seminar and the (indefensible) hour-long monologue, but it may be the case that for certain disciplines and in certain situations this compromise is acceptable.

It has, however, certain drawbacks. A disconcertingly large proportion of the students will assume that when the formal lecture finishes, the session is effectually ended. They make this assumption regardless of the teacher's earlier recommendation that the concluding discussion should be regarded as an integral part of the session and may well prove just as instructive as his lecture. As a result of this assumption, some students begin assembling their notes, some exchange a word with their neighbour and some prepare to take their leave. This makes it difficult for the teacher and the remaining students to concentrate and to hear what is being said. If at this point, the teacher raises his voice to assert his authority, the relaxed informal atmosphere is spoilt – and, in any case, those leaving or chatting are unlikely to desist. When questions are asked, and points made, during the actual course of the lecture, this is usually against a background of complete silence.

A second drawback is the fact, already referred to, that the best time to deal with a problem is when that problem arises in the mind of the student. If delay is imposed, he may lose interest or forget the question. At worst, he may not follow the latter part of the lecture, either because it seems to him (not necessarily rightly) that he lacks a vital link in the argument, without which the rest of the lecture cannot be understood, or because he is so intent on remembering and rehearsing his question that he is unable to take in the conclusion of the lecture. Thus, the solution of allowing a short time at the end of each session for public discussion is, in my view, not wholly satisfactory – though it is surely better than having no such discussion at all.

Till now, the direct benefit to the *student* has been stressed, but two-way communication is valuable also to the teacher – thus benefiting in addition future generations of students. If he has no immediate feedback, the lecturer does not know which aspects most interest his listeners, which prove most baffling, which stimulate them towards a new approach and which aspects, rightly or wrongly, they consider irrelevant. On this last point they may well be mistaken, but their teacher should be *aware* of what they consider irrelevant: he can then rethink, deciding either to abridge the offending section or to make a point of demonstrating its relevance. If he does not succeed in the latter course, the failure is his.

As a result of constant, though amiable, friction between keen, supple, young minds and his own, he learns to keep mentally alert, to maintain a healthy degree of self-criticism and to keep up with recent developments in his field. The insulation afforded by the dais and the one-way traffic of the formal lecture is rightly felt by him to be protective. If he is confident, however – and he can always remind himself that he probably knows more about the topic than anyone else in the hall – he will not need this protection and he will welcome a lowering of the 'I/they' barriers.

It is true that certain groups are more reticent than others. Some are unable, or unwilling, to respond to the invitation to participate, especially towards the beginning of the term. In that event the lecturer may need to be deliberately provocative in order to incite some member of the class into taking the first step. There are several possible procedures here. The teacher may simply adopt the course of posing a question to the class. This should be a rather general question to which correct/incorrect answers do not exist: a question asking for opinions rather than facts and, preferably, one on which passions run high. This sort of tactic is presumably easier in, for example, sociology than in pure mathematics.

Another strategy is to provoke by espousing somewhat extreme views. These are more likely to arouse opposition and, hence, participation from class members than are balanced, middle-of-the-road statements. If the discipline is scientific, it may be a question of selecting the evidence in a rather biased way – a course which is quite often taken, in any case, by scientists with an axe to grind (this phenomenon not being confined to the applied scientist!).

We are here faced with a genuine difficulty. I have suggested that the university teacher should aim above all to interest and stimulate his students, to challenge them mentally – in fact, to make them think. This is easily achieved, as stated above, by submitting extreme views and selecting unrepresentative conclusions. Yet it is equally important to be fair-minded, intellectually honest and to acknowledge several points of view. This problem can clearly not be solved by offering general rules. Perhaps all that can be suggested here is that the lecturer should periodically ask himself whether he is being too extreme for justice, too conservative to stimulate; and to reiterate that the best way to discover the answer to such questions is by exposing himself to the invigorating sallies of his students.

Chapter IV

Matter, manner and mannerisms

'On parle toujours mal quand on n'a rien à dire.'
                                                    VOLTAIRE

To attempt to offer guidelines to the potential lecturer concerning the matter and the manner of his lectures, seems ambitious to the point of absurdity. It may well be argued that the matter is determined by the content to be covered and that this, along with the title of the course, is the lecturer's task to determine: that he has probably been appointed precisely because of his expertise and interest in the particular topic (or topics) which he is to teach. Similarly with his manner: if he is not allowed to express his own individuality in the *how* of teaching, it may be argued, what will be left to distinguish one lecturer from another?

There is some substance in these allegations. I therefore envisage making only very general suggestions here, being well aware that matter and manner are often indissolubly linked and that both are intimately related to the relevant discipline. In the later part of the chapter, however, concerning the mannerisms of lecturers, I propose to be more specific and more dogmatic.

The recommendations in this book are intended primarily for the novice, the inexperienced university or college teacher. He will, if he is wise, prepare his lectures carefully, in advance. But, having prepared them, should he *read* them to his class? Or should he memorize and recite them, as one may memorize and recite someone else's poem? Or should he make notes, more or less fully, and speak from these? If we ask three lecturers, we may get three different preferences in reply, but if we ask three students – or indeed any number of attenders at a lecture, conference, meeting or speech-day – we are likely to receive the same response: it is more enjoyable, easier to follow, less soporific, if the lecturer speaks than if he reads. (The second choice, that of memorization and recitation, seems to combine the worst of all worlds. No case, therefore, will be made for it and it will not be referred to again.)

Reading aloud is an art in which few excel. The tendency among most lecturers who read out their material is to enunciate every sentence at the same speed and with the same cadence, to press on relentlessly with none of the natural breaks and pauses that occur in ordinary speech and – when they are giving the lecture for the sixth or the sixteenth time – *to sound* as though they have heard it all before, six or sixteen times. This has the effect of deadening even the most inspiring material. If the lecturer himself does not appear interested in what he has to say, he is unlikely to hold the interest of many members of his audience. It is readily observable that most people prefer to listen to themselves rather than to other people, and lecturers are no exception. The development of this trait in the lecturer may almost be regarded as an occupational hazard.

The university teacher who reads out his lectures will almost certainly have perpetrated them as a writer – not as a speaker. The drawbacks of this have already been outlined in Chapter II. Moreover, once he has got his lectures written out, or typed, word-for-word, he is less likely to consider changing them, amending them, bringing them up-to-date, than if they are in the form of notes, either on cards or looseleafed. There is much to be said for treating his material as ephemeral and flexible, and a great deal against regarding it as immutable.

Why then do so many lecturers and public speakers *read* what they have to say? As is to be expected with such a widespread phenomenon, the explanations are multifarious. I offer the following list, aware that it is probably not complete: lack of confidence, indolence – combined, interestingly enough, with a kind of conscientiousness – the advantage of rehearsability and, above all, a short memory of the effortful ennui of being at the receiving end of a communication which is read aloud.

For the novice, the thunder of a sudden silence in the course of his lecture strikes with horror. A deliberate pause to enable his students to exchange glances or catch up on their note-taking is one thing, but an involuntary silence is quite another. It may indicate – or produce – a momentary mental block on the lecturer's part; it usually sounds much more protracted in his ears than in those of his students; and he is therefore liable to feel that he has lost their attention, without necessarily having done so.

This, then, is one of the reasons for electing to write out one's lectures in full and read them aloud. It may be briefly described as lack of confidence and this is more often found in the uninitiated than the experienced lecturer. The latter may, however, decide to continue as he has done before: it is not uncommon to find grey-heads reading their lectures as a matter of habit rather than choice. By this time, it may be due to indolence. The complete lectures may originally have been diligently prepared and polished, requiring probably more time than is needed for simply getting out main headings. Preparation of one's first few courses of lectures takes an inordinate amount of time. But once they are on paper, to continue to use them, reading them aloud to one's students, is to take the line of least resistance. Hence the paradoxical combination of indolence and conscientiousness mentioned above.

A more positive reason for completing the lecture and reading it aloud is that it can, in this form, be rehearsed and accurately timed. The lecturer who speaks from notes can rarely estimate the length of his talk with the same exactitude. He may elaborate and illustrate a little more, or a little less, according to his mood during the lecture and – if he encourages contributions – according to the number and type of comments he receives. These cannot be predicted since they vary from group to group. As suggested earlier, many lecturers believe they are giving the best value if they speak steadily for 50–55 minutes and then sweep out; and they are more likely to achieve this aim if they rehearse, and then read resolutely through, their lecture.

I believe, however, that the main reason for reading lectures rather than speaking from notes is that the newly appointed lecturer, though probably young, has forgotten what it was like when – still younger – he sat and suffered at the feet of those teachers who first write out their lectures *in toto* and then read them aloud. This can be an instructive experience but it is very seldom a pleasurable one. Before delivering one's first lecture, reading aloud is usually seen as a lesser evil – and sometimes as a positive asset. In my view, the lack of spontaneity and of natural breaks, the non-invitation to students to participate, the frequent monotony and the inability of many a lecturer to raise his eyes from his script, render reading the less attractive delivery – however lacking in grace and fluency the speech may be of the lecturer who tries to talk informally but is unaccustomed to so doing in public.

Failure to meet the eye of his students is a common fault in young, and occasionally even in experienced, teachers. It reduces communication in several ways: first by impeding the task of the listener. It is easier for members of the audience to hear what is being said if they can see the teacher's face, partly because the sound will carry better to them and partly because the facial expression and lip-movements of the speaker provide additional clues to what he is saying. Cinema and television audiences have a startled awareness of this, whenever they see a badly dubbed foreign film.

Equally important, however, are the factors of rapport and of personal interest between teacher and taught. The lecturer cannot, of course, talk directly to every individual in his class but he can give the impression of so doing, by looking now to the far left, now the middle distance, etc. He will find not only that his listeners warmly appreciate this sign of humanity but that he gains in valuable feedback: he will find himself registering, 'this point is well-taken', 'he looks unconvinced', 'that puzzles them – I'd better elaborate', as he talks.

The lecturer who persists in keeping his eyes on his script or on the floor, gives an impression of contempt or embarrassment or unawareness of his audience. None of these inferred attitudes is popular with students and all repercuss on the speaker, whether or not he perceives it. If, as is likely with the reader of lectures, he does not invite comments and questions, he may well not realize the impression he is making throughout his career as a university teacher.

When we turn from 'manner' to 'mannerisms' we may be turning from the lecturer's individuality to his idiosyncrasies. On the whole, a strong individuality in a teacher is an asset, however it may manifest itself. Idiosyncratic mannerisms, however, are undesirable in a lecturer and should if possible be avoided. I have in mind such habits as nail-biting, head-scratching, nose-picking, hair-rumpling, striding rapidly from side to side of the platform, dropping cigarette ash down one's sleeve, compulsively rolling-up one's gown or other garments, affecting a stutter unnecessarily (particularly on the first person singular). I have met all of these mannerisms in lectures and it is quite possible that I have inflicted some of them on my own students, for it is clear to the observer that the lecturer is entirely unaware of what he is doing. One, otherwise admirable, lecturer of many decades back used to emit 'er' unwittingly, every four or five words. What he said was usually very interesting but his students were so busy counting his 'ers' (for purposes of the weekly sweepstake) that they missed a good deal of his excellent material.

This is a good example of the compulsive viewing or listening which

some mannerisms evoke in their audience. It is well for the teacher to be
aware early on of his particular singularities, whether visual or auditory,
because once such a habit has become ingrained it is extraordinarily
difficult to break. Many mannerisms, of course, are innocuous or may
even invest the teacher with a kind of trade mark which his pupils
enjoy. But those which either detract from what he is saying (such as the
er-counting phenomenon) or which are likely to prove actively dis-
tasteful (such as absent-minded ear-cleaning) should probably be
avoided. With the advent of feedback to lectures – which, it is to be
hoped is here to stay – unacceptable or distracting behaviour in a
teacher is less likely to arise and endure now than in the past.

Chapter V

Lecturing to the disabled

'The important thing in life is not what advantages
you begin with, but what handicaps you overcome.'
Jack ASHLEY (deaf) MP and author of *Journey into Silence*

My attention has been drawn to the fact that lectures are sometimes
given specifically for the disabled. The term here applies to the deaf, the
dumb, the deaf and dumb, and the blind. I am fortunate enough to have
been instructed on this topic by a very knowledgeable informant, Mr
Keith B. Poole, Hon. FHS.* Mr Poole is nearly blind, having a detached
retina in one eye and myopic degeneration of the visual nerve in both
eyes. He has given a highly successful course of lectures to the disabled
and he has been generous in passing on his recipe for success. It seems
worthwhile to include a chapter on this topic, for the following reasons.

First, most audiences include a few members whose vision or hearing
is less than adequate. Secondly, many student audiences today contain
immigrants and others whose English may be imperfect. Many of the
suggestions made below might well be of use to such students. Thirdly,
it may occasionally fall to the lot of a specialist in a particular discipline
to be asked to deliver a course of lectures to a disabled group. Indeed, it
is perhaps worth recording that Mr Poole – an experienced lecturer
living far afield – was requested to give a course of lectures (on heraldry) after several local university lecturers, well-qualified in this
topic, had declined the assignment.

Mr Poole accepted it. His audience consisted of 65 persons, all
interested in heraldry. All were partially or wholly blind, deaf or dumb –
some being both deaf and dumb. He delivered his lectures sitting on a
dais, which was sufficiently high for his head and shoulders to be

*Honorary Fellow of the Heraldry Society.

clearly visible from any position in the lecture hall. It is noteworthy that he *sat*, as it is usually assumed that greater clarity and authority are gained by standing, when lecturing. It was better for Mr Poole to sit, since being partially blind affects one's balance. But it is true also that sitting confers, for both lecturer and audience, an atmosphere of relaxedness and informality which is especially appropriate when the members of the audience are keenly interested in the topic and when all start out with a certain empathy with the speaker.

Mr Poole always pays great attention to the articulation of his words and the rhythm of his speech, and during these lectures he paid extra special attention to these. He also spoke deliberately slowly. A narrow pencil-beam of light was focused on his mouth. He was asked to remove his dark glasses in order that his eyes should be seen as clearly as possible.

On one side of Mr Poole sat an amanuensis, who wrote down his remarks, very clearly, as he uttered them. By means of an overhead projector these were magnified and projected on to a screen behind him, for the deaf to read. On his other side sat someone who repeated his words in silent lip language.

Thus the lecture was given simultaneously on three channels, analogous to the three or four channel simultaneous translation often used in international conferences – except that here the three languages used were for those who could read but not hear, could hear but not see and those who could lip-read but not hear. In fact this account over-simplifies the issue since some members of the audience gained some part of their information from two or even three of the different channels – being unable to gather the whole from any single channel.

The course was a great success. The jokes were understood and laughed at; the questions raised were numerous and very much to the point; the written work handed in afterwards was of a high standard. The audience contained very diverse people, some holding responsible posts. It was evident from the response that many were exceptionally able and that the majority had greatly benefited from the course.

For Mr Poole it was a deeply satisfying and moving experience. He was naturally delighted with the appreciation shown by his students and gratified to have succeeded in teaching them and stimulating them to further study in the field. But, in addition, he felt that an undertaking with dauntingly difficult obstacles had been fulfilled – an undertaking at which others had baulked. He, himself, felt that he had learned a good deal, as indeed one almost always does in the course of instructing students of any kind. Moreover, he felt inspired to take on further lecturing for the disabled.

This experience carries suggestions for teaching other disabled students, in addition to those with impaired vision and hearing. Many lecture courses include a few students who are physically disabled, owing for instance to polio or a spinal injury. And the facilities in many lecture halls could be improved if some thought were given to the problem while the building was being planned. The provision of ramps instead of steps, and lifts as well as staircases; the incorporation of wide gangways and corridors to accommodate wheel-chairs more easily; the eschewing of doors made entirely of glass, in any building likely to be used by the blind or partially blind; clear signs to indicate the direction of wide-doored cloakroom accommodation – these are a few obvious suggestions.

The disabled like to be able to participate in as many 'normal' activities as possible; they tend to be unusually highly motivated; and they prefer it if their handicap can remain unobtrusive. They are sensitive about their disabilities and hate to feel that they are causing extra trouble. Furthermore there is a kind of proliferation-effect: any one disability, whether sensory or motor, severe or slight, tends to place an additional burden on the other senses. For example, someone who usually wears spectacles is aware of having greater difficulty in hearing what people say, if he is for some reason deprived of his spectacles The need for the blind to heighten by every means their powers of hearing is well-known.

Thus attention should be paid to the disabled student, partly in his own right – because he needs every possible aid in getting the most out of his courses – and partly because most of us are potentially disabled in one way or another, especially as we grow older. I am not proposing that all teachers should have a beam of light directed towards their mouth or should be flanked by an amanuensis and a lip-reader! But I am proposing that this chapter suggests an additional reason for attending to all the techniques which contribute to the student's ease in following his lecturer.

Chapter VI

Two cultures?

'Unless you're a scientist, it is far more important for a
theory to be shapely than true.'

Christopher HAMPTON *The Philanthropist*

Arts/science is often regarded as a dichotomy. As with many apparent
dichotomies, however, the two elements here are more realistically seen
as lying on a continuum – with mathematics and the physical sciences at
one end and, say, literary studies at the other. The biological sciences are
habitually regarded as 'less scientific' than physics and chemistry,
largely because they are less strictly quantifiable and enjoy less precise
predictive power. And there are, of course, a whole host of disciplines
occupying – not always for the same reason – the middle ranges. Let us
call these, for future reference, the black swans. They include geo-
graphy, sociology, philosophy, social anthropology, economics and
others.

Some psychologists seek, and claim to find, essential differences
between artsmen and scientists, usually ignoring the black swans in the
process. That this belief is not confined to psychologists is shown by such
remarks as: 'She never has anything to say for herself – but then of
course she is a mathematician' or 'He makes the wildest statements,
quite unsupported by evidence – but perhaps this is normal in a poet'.
The man is the street – to say nothing of the woman – have their
stereotypes of science and arts no less than has the social psychologist.

That scientists and artsmen are not always essentially different
people, however, seems likely in view of the success of the multi-
disciplinary courses offered at many of the newer British universities
and also the relative frequency with which students – in their teens,
twenties or even thirties and forties – switch from one subject to

another, sometimes at opposite ends of the spectrum. Such individuals often prove exceptionally valuable members of their academic community.

There are certain differences, however, which are probably best described in terms of personal interest. This is no explanation: it is a factual description. The first part of this book has taken for granted many features in common between the scientist and the artsman. It has been assumed that the aims of the teacher are similar for both, that the same recommendations and caveats apply, that the students of whatever disciplines will all wish to learn, to assimilate, to criticize, to discuss and to think for themselves. Let us now consider whether there are any basic differences between the study of arts and the study of science (ignoring the black swans) which the teacher would do well to explore.

The first point to examine is the meaning and the place of *value judgments* in the two types of discipline. For the student reading natural sciences the question of values and tastes and opinions may well not obtrude itself at all, formally and at undergraduate level. If it does, it is likely to be in the form of assessing the appropriateness of evidence, the goodness of experimental design and the validity of proof and refutation. These are very special cases of value judgments. Whilst they may not be explicitly mentioned by lecturers, they implicitly underlie a good deal of what is taught, both in the physical and the biological sciences. In medicine, specifically, certain avowedly ethical and social values may form the subject matter of a few lectures at the clinical stage. But in his early days, the medical student – like the physicist, geologist and botanist – is busy assimilating facts, taxonomies and the objective relationships between them.

On the other hand, the arts student, during all his years at university if not earlier, is constantly urged to judge, to appraise qualitatively, to select from an *embarras de richesse et de pauvreté*. He is encouraged to form his own opinion and to express it vividly, forcefully, enterprisingly. It is not a question here of proof or disproof; matters of opinion are not demonstrable; questions of taste cannot be refuted. The successful arts student is original in his thinking; he is stimulating-or-dull rather than – like the future scientist – correct-or-incorrect. He capitalizes on his imagery – a mental process which is inevitably highly specific and personal. In a word, it is his job to be 'creative' from the time he embarks on his career as an artsman; and, nowadays, if he is 'creative' without keeping even one foot on the ground, he will be thought in some circles to be doing well.

This, surely, is one of the reasons why artsmen often do better on so-called 'tests of creativity' than do scientists. Many such tests favour the kind of imagination, totally unconstrained by reality, that is acceptable in some arts subjects. Creative imagination is indeed important also for the scientist but it tends to become relevant at a later stage in his career. Moreover, the advanced scientist's creativity generally needs to be within the bounds of established scientific fact. Thus the typical scientist in training cannot usefully offer new solutions to existing problems – let alone *ask new questions*, which is the ultimate for the scientist in research. But the confident young artsman can do both.

This leads to a second point of difference between arts and science, namely the immense amount of factual material which the student scientist has to master before it is worthwhile for him to begin speculating in his field. Formulating novel hypotheses, and toying with attractive-looking inventions, are worthless activities if the new ideas conflict with well-proven scientific laws. (Einsteins may constitute an exception to this but they, alas, come but once a century.) Despite the ever-increasing specialities emerging from the main body of science – colloid chemistry, bio-physics, molecular biology, computer science, psycho-pharmacology and bio-cybernetics, to name but a few from the last twenty years – the scientist must have a good background knowledge of general scientific fact before he can even begin specializing and he has also to keep up with recent discoveries in his own and related fields.

There is little comparable to this in the arts. Dissertations and books continue to proliferate, for instance, on Shakespeare, George Eliot and Milton. . . . And whilst it is desirable for the student of Shakespeare tragedies to know something about Shakespearian criticism, the main thing is to *know the plays* – and the number of plays he wrote has not increased since 1616. The Shavian saw, 'He who can, does. He who cannot, teaches' might be amended here to, 'He who can, writes; he who cannot, criticises'. Of course the ambitious arts student does have a great deal of reading to do. But good literature is not proceeding with the breathless speed at which the sciences are developing.

Furthermore, the artsman can devote all his working hours to reading, writing essays and attending lectures and tutorials. If he does talk shop with his friends (and some students do not) this is rightly regarded as a valuable adjunct to his work. The scientist has far less time to spend on these activities because – point 3 – he has to attend Practicals. This is a must, whether he is a physical or a biological scientist. The only exception is the mathematician.

Practicals tend to be frequent and time-consuming. To cut many is to incur the risk of dropping a class or division in the examinations and, more important, of creating startling lacunae in one's body of knowledge. The learning gained from practical classes is not identical with that gained from lectures and reading. It overlaps but it has a different flavour and sheds light on different aspects. As suggested above, comprehensive knowledge of one's subject in the sciences is more vital, and also more difficult to acquire, than it is in the arts. For some science students the very fact that the results of their practical experiments are known beforehand, divests them of glamour if not actually turning them to drudgery. This certainty of the more basic sciences is lacking in the arts and this lack may well be, to some, one of the attractions of the arts. Indeed it may be a contributory cause to the current school-leavers' drift away from science.

A fourth difference between arts and science is the strong element of the 'here and now' in most of the sciences. History of science is an accredited discipline in some universities but it is not regarded by staff or students as 'a science': it belongs with other histories and with philosophy rather than with chemistry, physiology or metallurgy. An able student of science, whether pure or applied, can do well if he concentrates on what is currently accepted in his field. He may even be encouraged to look to the future, particularly in areas such as ecology and computer science. But scientific theories and practices which have, by common consent, been superseded will not be taught in science courses.

On the other hand a historical viewpoint must be cultivated to some extent in the arts partly because it is an essential part of the culture which the arts teacher wishes to introduce to his students. It is necessary also for another reason: what is considered fine in the arts is what has stood the test of time. Fashions come and go with alarming speed and dogmatism in the arts. What is 'in' today may be 'out' tomorrow and what is new today may be acclaimed by Professor Scarlett and contemptuously rejected by Dr Chrome.

This is much less true in science. Fashions do occasionally play a part, especially in the biological sciences, but less capriciously and erratically than they appear, to the uninitiated, to do in the arts. Since the latter are so much concerned with value judgments, their teaching of contemporary studies is bound to contain a strongly subjective element.

Finally there is a greater emphasis on comprehension in science than in the arts. The science student is aware that he cannot get very far if he does not understand (as well as remember) what he is taught. He has to learn certain facts but knowledge of isolated facts is of little use to him. He needs to understand how they are related to one another. Above all, he has to learn to recognize and admit when he does *not* understand. This is less true of the artsman. He may be told with regard to a particular poem or play: 'It means whatever you make of it' or 'Just relax – the appeal here is to your emotions rather than your thoughts'. And sure enough, when a new play is reviewed in the press, three top critics may give three utterly different interpretations of it – and the playwright is quite likely to offer a fourth or to deny that interpretation is necessary or relevant to his work.

Five suggested differences between arts and science have been offered, deliberately omitting all reference to the black swans – which may be said to have a webbed foot in both camps. The differences described are probably controversial and surely not comprehensive. Let us nevertheless consider how such differences may affect the teaching of arts and sciences, respectively.

If it is true that values and taste play a greater role in the humanities, then it follows that the arts lecturer is concerned largely with making statements of an essentially individualistic position. If what he says is true for himself, he and his students can be satisfied. If, in addition, he puts it well, they should be delighted. In the arts, the 'how' of self-expression is as important as the 'what' and most expression is, indeed, expression of a personal attitude though it may on occasion appear less egocentric.

This does not apply to the teacher of science. If something of himself filters through into his lectures, in addition to the objective information he purveys, this may be regarded as something of a bonus (or quite the reverse, if what comes through is unattractive). In any case, it is much less relevant than it is in the arts, when the personality of the lecturer and his literary convictions may be inextricably mixed. Thus the *style* of the arts lecturer, along with his own particular ethos, politics and aesthetic sense, is crucial.

How about the vast body of factual knowledge with which the contemporary science student has to familiarize himself? A great deal of this is best acquired through books, journals and practicals. The task of the lecturer is here to guide his students' reading, to keep them up-to-date with the latest developments which are sometimes not yet readily available and to be on hand to answer questions and discuss problems which may arise in the course of these studies.

The arts teacher may claim that his students have actually far *more* reading to do, and this may be true in the sense of the number of volumes to be digested by the keen student of the humanities – perhaps in more than one language. But the arts student who is not keen can gain his third class on relatively sparse reading; he can, if he wishes, read extremely selectively; and sometimes he acquires sufficient ideas at second-hand. The scientist, on the other hand, must master his substantial minimum of information.

The organization of practicals is quite a vital feature in the teaching of science. The students usually work in pairs, the instructor often being oblivious of the importance of the relationship between the members of the pair. It is a highly skilled task to ensure that everyone knows what is required of him in a practical, that he sees the point of it and, if possible, that he gains enjoyment as well as instruction from it. Yet often the administration of practical classes is delegated to young, inexperienced research students, brilliantly qualified in their field and well able to cope with complex apparatus, but without so much as a preliminary discussion on the best way to deal with the human beings. Thus the vicious spiral continues. Those students who are most able – and hence, most self-sufficient – may derive pleasure and learning from practicals, whilst those who are confused and bored are likely to have similar partners and, gradually, to cut down on attendance.

The nearest approach to a practical in the humanities is perhaps the 'practical criticism', or the unseen translation, or the 'creative writing' class which we are importing from the USA. These differ from the science practicals in that the student works as an individual, not a member of a pair; and if he does decide to cut these classes he can, unlike the scientist, catch up by working on his own. The elaborate paraphernalia of modern science has, as yet, no place in the humanities. The language laboratories and the video-tapes are not really comparable with the centrifuges and the oscilloscopes, the cats and the cadavers, of the natural science practicals.

What I have listed as fourth and fifth – the 'here and now' of science and the necessity, at undergraduate level, for comprehension as opposed to imagination – may be discussed together from the teaching point of view. The scientist has to teach his students about the establishment of standards and 'laws' which are verifiable and public; measurement and precision are all-important; the student must learn how to manipulate and use certain concepts, most of which are operationally defined and, hence, are clear and relatively inflexible.

The artsman, however, has to learn to discover and then defend standards and points of view which are valid *for him;* quantification as such scarcely enters into the arts; precision may be called for in his mode of expression but he will sometimes wish to discuss a concept or a viewpoint which is shadowy or mutable or as yet dimly apprehended. The artsman is concerned with concepts in their own right, rather than with their manipulation and use. He has to learn that 'agreement to differ' is wholly acceptable, if not positively desirable, in certain arts situations whereas it is rarely acceptable in science as between teacher and undergraduate.

If we continue to ignore the black swans, can we find anything in common between the teaching of arts and of science – other than the suggestions made in the earlier parts of the book? I think that we can: that the first part of this chapter emphasizes, if not actually overstates, the differences. Both disciplines demand intellectual and emotional integrity on the part of the teacher. This requirement may be more obvious in the arts but it plays its role also in science, both pure and applied. In science this may take the form of admitting uncertainty or ignorance*, of presenting evidence which conflicts with the theory being propounded, of withholding judgment or of publicly changing one's mind.

In the arts, the matter is altogether subtler, since 'evidence' is often irrelevant and changing one's mind may conceivably produce a further book. Yet integrity is equally vital and, in both disciplines, students are apt to detect signs of its lack. They may not be able to pinpoint the problem but it may yet cause disquiet – and not the kind of disquiet which the teacher aims to arouse in his students. Perhaps the point is best made by deprecating the use of lectures for propagandising purposes, especially by the propagandist who implicitly assumes that the end justifies the means.

Another obvious shared feature is advice on reading. This is not just a matter of providing a booklist with suitably asterisked titles. Both the arts and the science lecturer should stress that their lectures are an addition to reading, not a substitute for it; that whilst the student needs to follow up many of the references given, he should also branch out

---

*I have noticed that when I make a mistake in a lecture, or discussion, it seems to have a mildly therapeutic effect.' P. C. WASON (1974), *Bull. Brit. Psychol. Soc.*, 27.

adventurously in pursuit of other books. Teachers could, moreover, well give advice on the different modes of reading: for instance, that certain books can be skimmed through, judiciously skipping here and there, and others need to be read and reread word-for-word — to say nothing of the books whose illustrations are better than the text, and conversely.

They should point out that quoting, either by heart or directly from the book, is no substitute for understanding and recapitulating in one's own words; and that the latter is infinitely the more valuable. Admittedly the artsman will be expected to read more books, faster, than the scientist – most of whose reading is more technical and harder to digest – but both need some guidance on their reading-matter and some reminder that no other medium can take the place of books and journals.

Let us finish where we began, on the question of value judgments – aesthetic, social, political and ethical. Whilst it is true that these have an obvious role to play in the arts, scientists themselves are becoming increasingly aware of their own power in the material – and indeed, the psychological – world. And the use of these powers implies certain values and disvalues. These are, of course, not intrinsic to the science which is taught at undergraduate level: they are extrinsic to it and refer essentially to the applied sciences.

The line is a fine one, however, between pure and applied, between intrinsic and extrinsic, between undergraduate and post-graduate work. As mentioned above, the physician-to-be receives some teaching in medical ethics, before he qualifies. We might also have mentioned the 'elegance' of proof, beloved of the mathematician and physicist, which yields them literally an aesthetic delight. All-in-all, the resemblances between the teaching of arts and of science probably outweigh the differences.

Chapter VII

The tutorial or supervision

Johnson: 'I had no notion that I was wrong or irreverent to my tutor.' Boswell: 'That, Sir, was great fortitude of mind.' Johnson: 'No, Sir, stark insensibility.'

Boswell's *Life of Johnson*

'Remember that every person, however low, has rights and feelings.'

Sydney SMITH

The weekly tutorial, or supervision, during term-time has long been a feature of Oxbridge undergraduate life, and the practice is growing in the newer universities. It usually takes place in the supervisor's study or lab-room and lasts for about an hour; its ratio is one staff member to one or two students, who generally produce a weekly essay on a topic chosen by the tutor. Most of the time is spent in discussing the essay and any problems which the student has encountered in the course of his work or of his university life generally.

This indicates the general theme – upon which many variations are played. The meetings may be less or more frequent than one per week, the 'staff member' may be a research student, the number of pupils is sometimes as many as three or four, the concept of 'hour' is highly flexible and so is that of the essay. This ranges from a 16-page manuscript or typescript, submitted two days in advance, to a half-page of scrappy notes which the students draws from his pocket during the session. The topic may be chosen by the pupil, or it may have been officially selected by the supervisor – the essay occasionally turning out to be on some quite other subject. Even the venue is not always as decorous as suggested above. Tutorials in pubs and cafés are not unknown; some tutors like to conduct their session against a background of music; and I know of one who occasionally supervises his students while (himself) in the bath.

Such vagaries seem to be independent of the particular faculty and also of the background and maturity of the student. Some students, clearly, are more sophisticated than others, especially in their first year, and some are better able to speak up for themselves, i.e. to protest if they feel that their needs are not being met in tutorials. This, however, is a tricky matter. When students first enter university, they do not know what to expect in the way of supervisions (or, indeed, of lectures). Various myths circulate. In some departments, for instance, students assert that the most important factor influencing their university career is their supervisor – some going so far as to attribute solely to him their prospective degree class. In other departments or at different times, students hold on the contrary that supervisions are largely a waste of time and as such should be avoided whenever possible.

The truth lies usually somewhere between these two extremes, the benefit gained by the pupil being largely determined by the relationship gradually established between him and his tutor. On this relationship, too, will depend the benefit gained *by the tutor* – for as in all teaching situations (except for 'teaching-machines') the learning is a two-way process. The supervisor will, if he has sufficient humility, add something to his knowledge of the relevant subject matter, for the student has a younger, sometimes a more critical, approach and is perhaps more accessible to new ideas. But the tutor has also the opportunity of learning something about human relations in general and about his own pupils in particular, if he is interested and open-minded enough to do so. Indeed, the latter is part of his job, for he will probably be asked to act as a referee when the student goes down and he will certainly have to send in a report, at the end of term.

Is it possible to formulate any general principles to guide the potential supervisor – bearing in mind the variety of personalities and disciplines involved – so that his pupils may derive the maximum gain from his tutorials? Perhaps the easiest way to achieve this is to look at the failures: to examine those supervisors who tend to be censured by their pupils, and to consider the reasons given by students for dissatisfaction. There seem to be four main sources of complaint: lack of interest, ignorance, intimidation and rigidity.

Some supervisors are occasionally not available to their pupils at the allotted time. When this occurs – in the absence of any explanation – it is apt to have a deflating and discouraging effect on the student. Sometimes the tutor is there but the essay, presented in advance, is unread, or even 'mislaid'. Such discourtesies are, admittedly, infrequent but they are not unheard of.

'He simply picked up my essay from the corner of his desk where I had put it and said, "I suppose this is all right – afraid I haven't had time to read it".' The expression on the face of the student who told me this was unforgettable. He was a gifted and conscientious economist (now a Fellow of an Oxford college) – and he was still shocked, weeks after the occurrence. This action – or inaction – of the tutor is inexcusable, whether it be due to bad timing on his part, sheer forgetfulness, pressure of other work, or the conviction that this particular student knows his stuff and can safely be left to get on with it. Said, with neither apology nor intention to make amends, it is breaking faith with his pupil and his job. It implies a depressing apathy with regard to his discipline, and of course to his pupil as a person and as a potentially serious student.

The case is rather different when, the pupil having been asked to write an essay on whatever aspect of the subject he chooses, the supervisor says: 'I haven't read this because you've chosen a topic I know nothing about'. One instance of precisely this reaction was brought to my notice by a student of psychology at London University some years ago. She was given a free choice; she elected to write on the EEG; and when she came to discuss the essay she was greeted with the remark quoted above.

This does show some lack of interest and energy, for the tutor could surely have consulted the literature or have found some colleague with knowledge of the EEG to read the essay and comment on it. But what is self-indicting is his ignorance: he was evidently unaware that he needed to limit his pupil's choice of essay subject. Some students enter university with the belief that their teachers are omniscient, at least in their own field. They fairly swiftly come to realize that this is not so and this realization may well be salutary and even encouraging to them. But they dislike a concealment of ignorance in their teacher – a pretence of knowledge where it is lacking.

They will sometimes even set schoolboy traps for this. One of my students put into his essay an esoteric reference – complete with name and date – which was new to me. When I expressed interest in this, he laughingly admitted that he had made it up. Thereafter, however, he desisted from this practice.

Indifference and ignorance (especially of recent developments) are more likely to be found in elderly tutors, who have been supervising for many years than in young dons or – even younger – research students. The latter tend to be knowledgeable, up-to-date with current theory and practice, grateful for the experience of teaching and keen to prove themselves worthy of the trust – and the supervision fees. But they are quite often unwittingly intimidating. They are liable to turn the full blast of their newly-acquired expertise on to their pupils, to demand highly specialized material even from their first- and second-year students and to concentrate on the informational aspect of the supervision, entirely ignoring its pastoral aspect.

Some junior students are easily frightened; they timidly accept the very high intellectual level set by their tutor who, unlike them, will probably be an academic all his life; they become scared when they find they cannot live up to his standard; they grow to dread each session and, hence, each essay-writing. This of course makes them appear far less able, on paper and in person, than is the case. A vicious circle may then be set up which, every week, becomes increasingly difficult to break. It may even contribute occasionally to a psychiatric breakdown.

This is particularly likely to happen if their supervisor is both brilliant and caustic. The following two incidents are drawn from life; word-for-word accounts of how two tutors enraged and offended their respective pupils – an excellent recipe for producing the frustration which leads to breakdown. In case 1, the student was set an essay on Delinquency. A conscientious young man, taking himself and his work rather seriously, he asked for references. 'Oh, just introspect!' was the only reply he received. Being sensitive to the point of touchiness, he did not perceive this as humorous – merely as offensive. In case 2, the sole comment the student obtained on his essay was that it was 'a load of undigested vomit'. This particular student did become a psychiatric case – evidently helped in this direction by his singularly unimaginative supervisor.

There are not many sadistic tutors – although academics generally are of course the kind of people whose natural aggression tends to express itself in an articulate and intellectual form. But there are quite a few who unnerve their students, simply because they assume too early that tutor and pupil are speaking the same language and that if the student cannot keep up, it is his own fault. It does not occur to some tutors that they may be making too great demands of their pupils, too soon. Moreover, they often concentrate exclusively on the subject matter of the tutorials, not realizing the need to build up a reasonably warm relationship at the same time.

Indeed, for some pupils, the weekly supervision may go beyond normal pastoral care and provide a positive, sometimes necessary, therapeutic situation, particularly in cases where the student does not see eye to eye with his 'moral tutor'. or when the latter is often unavailable. There are some ways in which the supervision is analogous to the session of psychotherapy: the regularity and frequency of meeting, the one-to-one relationship (when the pupil is supervised on his own), the dependency of the student during the period that he is learning to stand on his own feet, and the fact of sharing a common task which requires that each shall get to know the strengths and weaknesses of the other.

If the tutor constantly offers criticism of a destructive kind, this is experienced by the student as rejection and it is unlikely to help him much in his work. It should usually be possible to find some redeeming features in a poor essay or a dull discussant. The supervisor who fails to do so is very likely reflecting some failure in himself. He may lack the self-confidence or the generosity to discover merit in others. Or he may be too rigid to remould his tutorials in a way which better suits his pupil. Too many supervisors have a fixed plan of how to run their supervisions, holding the view that the task of adaptation is wholly the student's.

For instance, one such tutor complained to me: 'He sat in silence for over a quarter of an hour. He just couldn't think of anything to say.' It did not, apparently, occur to him that this could be quite demoralizing for his pupil, if not wholly traumatic; that the onus of breaking the silence was, at the very least, *shared* by them both; and that an unwilling, barren silence is time wasted. On the other hand, toleration of an occasional, brief silence should be acquired, to allow both to collect their thoughts, if necessary, and to enable the pupil to 'screw his courage to the sticking point'. should he need this. Neither should feel that a momentary pause is to be avoided at all costs, but it is the tutor's task to ensure that such silences are experienced as *relaxed*.

Rigidity on the supervisor's part may take the form then of providing a procrustean framework into which the mentally tall and short, slender and thickset, are required to fit. Even the way to terminate a tutorial may provide anxiety: more than one student has lamented to me that his teacher 'has no idea how to end the session' and supervisors will often complain of a pupil that he 'does not know when to leave'. Such a deadlock is apt to result in feelings of resentment on both sides. Again, it seems to me, the member of staff should accept responsibility – in this case for ending the supervision; and evidently the inexperienced and shy tutor could do with a few hints in this regard.

If merely rising to his feet does not evoke a similar response from the student, the supervisor may say: 'Is there anything else?' or 'Any further points?' This may evoke an immediate retreat on the pupil's part or, on the contrary, may elicit a flood of confidences which the student needs to get off his chest. Surprisingly often, the most crucial part of a supervision is crowded into the last 5–10 minutes of the session.

If the pupil remains seated or fidgets indecisively, evidently unsure whether to go or to stay, a brisk but smiling 'See you next week' or 'Well, I think that's all' will usually solve his problem – and his tutor's. If possible, the pupil should feel cheered on leaving. As one student put it when discussing a term of successful tutorials: 'I always felt twice as clever when I left than when I arrived [at the supervision].'

The above discussion has assumed that the tutorial comprises one staff member and one pupil. This ratio, however, is becoming rarer as student numbers expand and financial resources shrink. (The smaller the number of pupils in a supervision group, the greater the expense to the college, per student.) There are advantages in the one-to-one ratio: the pace can be adjusted to the individual, if the supervisor is sufficiently perceptive; the tutorials can be tailored to fit the particular academic *interests* of the student, a judicious compromise being reached between the requirements of the syllabus and the intellectual leanings of the pupil; 'problem children', whilst they may trouble the tutor, will not upset fellow pupils; and a closer acquaintanceship is of course set up in a group of two than a group of three or four.

There are other advantages, however, in supervising two or more pupils in the hour. The most obvious is that this is less time-consuming for the tutor than taking students singly, although of course no time is saved in the actual reading of essays, if this is done in advance – a practice, in my opinion, to be followed. If essays are read aloud during the tutorial, very little time is left for discussion. There are also some advantages for the students, especially the more reserved ones, who are often more willing to discuss and to argue with one another than they are, at least initially, with their supervisor. Moreover, in a group of two or three, they become closely acquainted with the written work of their peers; they learn of the different interpretations which may be made of the essay title; and they appreciate the strength and weakness of points which would perhaps never have arisen in a consideration of their own essay, alone.

When two pupils supervising together elect to write essays on different subjects, it is wise to ensure that each reads the other's essay before handing it in. In this way, a good deal of useful ground can be covered in the one seminar. The choice of type of tutorial should depend on the individual students and on the facilities of the university department.

Increasingly often, nowadays, students request a very few highly specialized tutorials, from university teachers in their own particular field of research. This is perhaps more likely to occur in the sciences than in the humanities. Thus in experimental psychology, for instance, a student may ask for two supervisions in psycholinguistics, two in intelligence testing, two in experimental design and two in learning theory – from, respectively, a psycholinguist, a psychometrist, a statistician and a learning theorist – instead of having eight supervisions (on these or other topics) from the same experimental psychologist. The latter – whatever his speciality – should be able to cope with these and other topics, and to advise on the relevant reading, although he will clearly not be able to supervise in the same depth as can an expert in one of these particular fields.

I think that this development is a pity: that the purpose of tutorials is to give the student the opportunity of getting to know a staff member, and to enable the staff member to get to know the student and his interests, his capacity for self-expression on paper and in person, his vocational ambitions, and also to appraise his work-potential generally. This requires at least one term of continuous supervisions with the same tutor. Extreme specialization is unnecessary, and even undesirable, until the student has a reasonable background knowledge of the whole field. If he is keen enough on some special aspect he can read concentratedly – which may indeed be better for him than being exposed early to a specialist who may be too deeply involved with his own original research on his topic to give an unbiassed picture. Moreover, if the tutor supervises exclusively in his own field, he tends to go stale – a state of affairs as distressing for his pupils as it is for himself.

A further reason for staying with the same supervisor for a term, or even an academic year, is that the student will in due course probably be applying for references, when seeking a job or further training, and it is impossible to make a serious assessment based on a mere two or three essays and discussions. It is not always easy to convince the eager student of the weight of these arguments and, too often, his teachers take the line of least resistance and agree to give him two (or even one) tutorial in depth, on some highly specialized topic. The student may regret this policy in his last term or when he has left the university, but by then it is, of course, too late.

To sum up: the giving of weekly supervisions or tutorials to one pupil, or to very small groups, is usual at Oxbridge. In general the students welcome the system – whatever form it may take – and the practice is growing in the newer universities. Many of those which began by instituting biggish seminars are now reducing the numbers of students in a group; and groups of three or four pupils are not unknown. These are very similar in aim and in effect to the tutorial or supervision. The limits are set rather by the total staff/student ratio in the Department than by the willingness of staff members to accept the one-to-one teaching situation.

The form varies even within a single institution or Department and this is highly desirable, since the students naturally vary in their needs, wishes and abilities. If a student expresses a desire for a particular form of tutorial, for example to supervise with a fellow-student – perhaps a friend of his choice – his wishes should be respected (providing of course that, in this instance, the friend welcomes the idea). If, however, his wishes cannot be met, the reason for this should be explained. The great virtue of the supervision system is that staff and student meet as equals, unseparated by platform or large numbers, in an atmosphere that is almost intimate – and that each has the opportunity of learning from the other.

Chapter VIII

Booklists and handouts

'Suggestive Book-list for Animal Psychologists' – heading of Notice posted in Psychology Department of University of Stanford, California, in the 1950s.

Many booklists offered to students are regarded by them as unsatisfactory: the lists are too long, or too short, out-of-date, insufficiently annotated. It is usual for university teachers to produce a reading list, whether in their capacity as lecturer, supervisor or director of studies. Selecting the titles is a harder task than appears at first sight, partly owing to the erudition of the teacher (he has to choose a few seminal books and articles from his wide reading, over many years) and partly owing to the diversity of the students. These range from able, zealous, future researchers to the carefree and not over-gifted, who aim to do the minimum of academic work which will yield them a third class degree. Not all booklists, moreover, are prepared with the same purpose in mind. Here, as elsewhere, the futility *of generalizing* is apparent – yet the whole of this book constitutes, in a sense, an attempt to generalize.

Some teachers will include as many as 40–50 titles, oblivious of the fact that many students find this length discouraging and that colleagues will also be offering lists to the same students. When challenged, they tend to say either that it is absolutely essential to read every item listed in their subject or to assert that the student is free to make his own choice from the list. In fact, producing too long a list demonstrates a kind of mental laziness: the list-maker finds it too much trouble to go through the titles carefully, eliminating those which are less important or those whose subject matter overlap substantially with one another. The phenomenon is similar to that of writing an unnecessarily long book or paper, owing to unwillingness to prune it in the early stages. Occasionally, undue length stems from the teacher's eagerness to keep the list up-to-date. He periodically adds new titles but omits to delete some of the early ones which may by this time have been superseded.

The effect of one or more over-long series of titles on the less secure student can be overwhelming. Sometimes he feels so daunted that he ignores the booklist completely. It is as though he argued, 'Since I can't possibly read the whole lot, it's not worthwhile reading any of them'. The more mature will perhaps discuss the problem with their supervisor (probably learning, in the process, how subjective is the choice of titles in a reading list) or they may indeed make their own selection, being guided by the names of the books and the authors.

Some teachers, aware of the dangers of producing too long a reading list, go to the other extreme and list a mere handful of titles. This again is to be deprecated, partly because – despite disclaimers in small print – the student is liable to think that if he reads those few he need explore no further in the relevant literature, and partly because such a short list offers too little in the way of *choice*. Student days are ideally a time of mental exploration, as well as a time 'to stand and stare'. The reading lists should be long enough to yield a choice, to tempt the student to explore some byways whose existence he knew nothing of – led to, perhaps, by books which may be relegated to rather obscure parts of his favourite library.

It is suggested above that students pay little heed to 'the small print'. They do, however, attend to symbols placed against the titles, if such symbols indicate for instance 'essential introductory reading', 'elaboration of lectures', 'useful reference book', 'for third year students'. These, or other, guides help to split up the list of 10–20 titles which I suggest is the length to aim at; they also help the young student to get his reading into perspective.

Perspective is needed also by the teacher. He should realize that it is imperative for his pupils that the relevant libraries should have sufficient copies of recommended books or that the books recommended should exist in paperback editions. Most people find it pleasantest to read their own books in their own room, but exceedingly few students nowadays can afford to buy hardbacks. Even those few who can do so, are sometimes frustrated since the local bookshops have not always been informed of key titles. Thus a delay of several months is not unknown – when the student orders a book from the bookshop and the shop, too late, orders it from the wholesalers.

Departmental libraries and college librarians often have only two copies of a crucial book, wanted perhaps by a score of students simultaneously. In these circumstances, 'one out and one missing' is a sadly frequent librarian's report. There is a widespread feeling among university teachers in both the arts and the sciences that students read less than they used to do. The blame is placed variously on schools, on television and on 'the different class of student' now coming up to the universities. These may all be blameworthy but some of the trouble may well be due to the manifold difficulties of actually obtaining copies of the requisite books or journals just when they are wanted.

It is a good idea to reserve a section of the departmental library for books which are important and popular, and which do not exist in paperback. Books in this section may not be removed: they must be read in the library. This system has the advantage that no one individual can monopolize a particular book for a whole term and it also reduces the risk of loss and theft. The continuous presence of an alert librarian, during the hours that the library is open, is indispensable.

A 'suggestion book' is a highly desirable adjunct to any library. Readers should be encouraged to give the titles of any additional books or journals which they would like the library to include and also to suggest any changes in administration, seating, opening-hours, etc., which they think would prove beneficial. They must be convinced – with reason – that the contents of the suggestion book are actually read at least once a term and that serious suggestions are seriously considered. The formation of a small library committee, comprising staff, research students and undergraduates, is probably the best way of ensuring that good service in this sphere is both achieved and seen to be achieved.

One or two lectures on library resources and the way to make best use of them might save students a good deal of time and trouble. Such teaching could include, for instance, the use of cross-reference material, how to locate titles and authors and how to make use of relevant journals and abstracting services. Such instruction would be particularly useful for first-year students – who may otherwise remain unaware of those facilities which the university libraries afford, beyond what is offered in most school libraries.

This chapter is an appropriate one in which to discuss also the question of handouts. These consist of abstracts or synopses of the lectures, distributed usually at the beginning of the lecture course – though some teachers prefer to issue them at weekly or fortnightly intervals throughout the term. They may or may not include a reading list.

Such handouts are often requested by the students on the grounds that they like to know what the course will cover and they feel that they are in a better position to enjoy the lectures if they have some background knowledge. Some students, however, decide on the basis of the handouts whether or not to attend the course. Those who decide against attending, do so either because they find the contents of the handout unattractive or 'irrelevant' (to their interests or their syllabus) or because they think that, having read the handout, they are now familiar with the substance of the lecture course.

I strongly believe in lecture attendance being optional. The bodily presence of a comatose student at a lecture confers no benefit on him, his fellows or his teacher. Some good students attend very few lectures – though this may well imply strictures on the lecturers, rather than an intrinsically greater merit in other modes of instruction. If the lectures are good enough, the student will read *and* attend lectures (and tutorials). As suggested in the earlier chapters, these ought to supplement one another: to fulfil different, but equally important, functions. Lectures which are stimulating and challenging, and which purvey material that has not yet found its way into the textbooks and journals, tend to be well-attended throughout the term.

For those courses in which student participation is invited, handouts at the beginning of term are particularly useful. They serve two purposes: first, as with other courses, they inform the student of the types of topic to be covered; secondly, they offer some indication of the sorts of question and comment which may pertinently be raised during the lectures – though not necessarily arising directly from any one given lecture. If public discussion is lively and the teacher for this reason does not reach the end of his lecture notes, the students will still have some idea of the subject matter which would have been covered and this may provide food for thought, for further reading, or discussion with fellow students.

As with booklists, there is a suitable length for handouts and also a suitable degree of information-level. Lest these points be thought too obvious to be worth stating, I should like to quote from a contemporary student (Gray of engineering). 'Dr Jet produced a handout of *75 pages*' said Gray bitterly 'and then his lectures turned out to be on something quite different!' Gray grinned at his own account but it was a wry grin. 'It's so dishonest', he continued, 'either Jet should have given *two* courses or he should have admitted that his so-called "handout" was the draft of a book'.

This true story illustrates several points. University students are, for the most part, prepared to read the writings of their teachers but they object to being misled. Notes designated as a handout for a lecture course should be brief – not usually exceeding two or three pages – and should be closely related to the actual course. They should be informative as to the subject matter but it is unwise to reveal, however briefly, just what conclusions will be reached. Thus, to take an example from physiology, 'the results are discussed in terms of a division of function within the inferotemporal region of the brain' is preferable to 'the results implicate the anterior and posterior portions of the infero-temporal region of the brain, in memory and perception, respectively'.*

If the latter form is used throughout the handout, some students will feel that they have learned little more from attending the lecture than they had learned from reading the handout, and others may – perhaps misguidedly – elect to cut the lectures.

To sum up, booklists and preliminary handouts are important adjuncts to university teaching. If they are not provided, students tend to demand them. If they are forthcoming, the students are in general appreciative – providing that they fulfil reasonable expectations respecting length, information-level and relevance. The wants of students are changing, perhaps faster than are the methods of university instruction. The university teacher, rather than sitting back complacently, needs to be on his toes. It is possible to appraise one's effectiveness, and to discover one's weak points as a teacher, if 'feedback' is used. This useful technique is discussed in Chapter XIII.

---

*I am indebted to Dr Trevor Robbins for this example.

Chapter IX

Teaching versus research

'To my electron: may no-one find any use for it!'
J. J. THOMSON, *circa 1900*

Since this whole book deals with teaching and its objectives, no attempt will be made to define what is meant by 'teaching'. It should already be evident that the word has different connotations for different university teachers and also for different disciplines. Since, however, this chapter is concerned with the relationship between teaching and research, and the possibility that either may be pursued to the detriment of the other, it may be desirable to discuss what is meant by the term 'research' and what are the aims of this activity.

We are liable to encounter some of the problems met with in Chapter VI, where an endeavour was made to find some meeting ground of the arts and the sciences without leaning so heavily on the 'black swans' that they sank without trace. It is likely that certain basic differences obtain between the research of artsmen and that of scientists. The issue is perhaps further complicated by the distinction between pure and applied research in the sciences – or does this distinction apply also in some of the arts ?

To consider the pure/applied question first: this dichotomy, like so many, appears on reflection to be one of degree rather than of kind. Theoretical discussion which attempts to draw the line between the pure-and-basic on the one hand and the specific-and-practical on the other, soon leads either to an insoluble argument or to agreement that 'fundamental' project x may be found to stir up just as much mud – or gold-dust – as does 'applied' project y.

In this form, the idea is stated as an abstraction. But the statement does have empirical truth in that many pieces of work which started as basic, theoretical or pure research have turned out rapidly to have practical application. In other cases the time-lag is longer, but the practical uses still do eventually reveal themselves. The converse is also true: many pieces of research embarked upon in an *ad hoc* way, to solve some highly specific practical problem have turned out, sometimes unpredictably, to have general implications of long-lasting theoretical value.

Let us illustrate this with two examples, (a) from the physical sciences – a piece of research originally conceived as basic, turning out to have innumerable applied uses; and (b) from the biological sciences – where what began as very practical research acquired considerable theoretical importance.

(a) began with the theory that light and electric waves are forms of electromagnetism – and ended (if that is the correct word) with the vast radio industry. James Clerk Maxwell, British Scientist, 1831–79, developed the equations, well known to physics students, which implied that high-frequency (electric) currents would radiate waves. In 1886, Heinrich Hertz, German physicist, 1857–94, demonstrated experimentally the existence of these waves. He showed that electric waves, in their susceptibility to reflection, refraction and polarisation, correspond precisely to the waves of heat and light.

These two theorists (along with others, such as the chemist, Faraday) paved the way for the practical possibilities of 'wireless telegraphy'. Gugliemo Marconi, Italian scientist, 1874–1937, applied their principles in order to invent/discover what is now called 'radio'. In 1901, Marconi sent the first wireless signal across the Atlantic. The practical applications of radio were already immense in the 1930s. With the advent of World War II, however, these ramifications – as in so many scientific spheres in war-time – very swiftly proliferated. They now include colour television, microwave communication – and ovens; chemical analysis by nuclear magnetic resonance; radar – not forgetting the speed-trap.

This particular example, as presented above, is inevitably oversimplified. There were other precursors to Marconi – and he, on the other hand, may be said to share the honours with Popov. Moreover, the theoretical and the applied often interweave with each other a good deal. The example is nonetheless a useful one in that it illustrates several points, of which non-scientists may not always be fully aware. The first of these is the *international* quality of science. Secondly, the advance of a branch of science *over a long period of time* is manifest, this advance sometimes proceeding by fits and starts. Lastly, the tremendous fillip effected by *war* is evident; this phenomenon, interestingly, is shared by the arts, including the fine arts.

Example (b), drawn from biology, illustrates a change of emphasis in the other direction: it begins with the practical, medical problem of treating pneumonia and ends with the theory of DNA. It should be stressed that this epoch-making theory, too, was not nourished – as the following paragraphs may suggest – by only one stream. Most, if not all, important theories are sustained by several tributaries. But what follows is generally accepted, in this instance, as a major river.

Until the discovery of the sulphonamides, the pneumococcous was a very dangerous organism. Research workers in the field of public health conducted many studies on its epidemiology, including work on its variations in virulence, with the idea of preventing the infections that could not always be cured. Griffith's paper of 1928, from the Ministry of Health Pathological Laboratory, was one such study. He found, among other results, that when living pneumococci of a non-virulent strain were injected into a mouse, together with killed pneumococci of a virulent strain, virulent bacteria appeared and could be propagated. The search for the nature of the transforming factor which the dead bacteria passed to the living took fifteen years. It culminated in a paper by the American scientists, Avery, McLeod and McCarty in 1944, adducing powerful evidence that the factor was DNA.

Chromosomes had long been known to contain DNA. They also contain protein – which was the obvious candidate for the role of the genetic material carried by the chromosomes, because protein had the enormous potential for variety of structure that the genes must possess. The paper by Avery and his colleagues was the first clear indication that DNA, transferred from one organism to another, could induce a change that was henceforth inherited. As a result, the attention of a few scientists, encouraged also by some later evidence in the same direction from virology, turned strongly to DNA. Ten years later, the Watson-Crick model solved the problem of how DNA could contain a vast wealth of information, and how it could replicate in the way required for heredity: and a great theoretical revolution in biology followed.

This example, only slightly less international in flavour, again illustrates progress over many years, seemingly proceeding in a stop-go manner, though the latter may be more apparent than real. The DNA story exemplifies also the scientific importance of *teamwork* – an importance which is constantly increasing and is probably more crucial in the sciences than in the arts.

These illustrations are far from unique. Indeed, such instances are repeatedly found in the history of science. Moreover, the pure-to-applied phenomenon is not confined to the physical (or border-zone) sciences nor is the applied-to-pure transformation limited to biological and allied fields.

If it be agreed, then, that the distinction between pure or fundamental research, on the one hand, and applied or practical research, on the other, is one of degree rather than kind, we can explore the general question of 'what is research?' hoping to find certain features in common among all research work. University teachers are well aware of the difficulties of communicating the meaning of the term to students who are wondering whether 'to go into research' or who, already committed for at least three years, are trying to find out what it is that they are committed to. It is essentially an activity which one understands only by doing. One embarks, sometimes impetuously, sometimes hesitantly, on the confusions and frustrations of one's first research project, often uncertain of the questions to be asked, the relevant methods of inquiry and, above all, of recognizing the answers.

Researching is a one-step forward, half-step-back, mode of progression – when all goes well – a process of lifting oneself by one's bootstraps; it is both glamourous and pedestrian, inspired and meticulous, requiring wide vision and obsessional perseverance. It can be endlessly stultifying and endlessly rewarding; it is demanding yet needs great freedom – to take a chance, to lie fallow, to try again. One must be able to see the wood for the trees but to concentrate on the wood to the exclusion of the trees is to court disaster. It is an insecure way of life and yet, when once embraced, it is curiously difficult to extricate oneself. How can this strange amalgam be convincingly described to the undecided student? And how far should the description take the form of propaganda of an encouraging nature? How far, on the contrary, should the snags be clearly represented?

It is not only that the discovering aspect of research tends to be romanticized and misunderstood by those in other walks of life. They are apt also to forget that this aspect is only one of many stages: that choosing an area and identifying a problem within it usually precedes the discovery stage and that analysing the results, evaluating them and writing them up, constitutes the final, necessary stage. Some pieces of research never reach a satisfactory conclusion because the original question is ill-put – and the research worker or his director seem unable to rethink the early formulation; and many an initially promising piece of research is marred by the confused or misleading way in which it is written up. A surprisingly large number of research workers lose interest when the writing-up stage has been reached – even if the results are pleasing. They do not see this as a stage *in research* at all, finding the earlier, discovery phases infinitely more exciting.

These phenomena make for two effects. First, different university teachers tend to look for very differing qualities in their potential research students. Thus, Mrs Black regards intellectual brilliance and flair as the *sine qua non* for anybody to be considered for a research grant. On the other hand, Professor Maroon writes in a reference: 'Once he gets going, he would show enterprise, diligence and determination. Such people, in my experience, often turn out more satisfactory research students than many with greater intellectual range or brilliance'. And Lord Fawn stresses the fact that his particular protegé possesses the gifts of critical sense and lucid exposition, essential to a successful dissertation. In effect, a blend of all these qualities is needed for fruitful research, and the fact that many applicants for research grants have only one or two such traits may account for the distressingly high number of theses, in all disciplines, which should never have seen the light of day.

The attitude of university teachers used to be that only the very exceptional student who combines the above gifts with a strong urge to carry out research, should be encouraged to do so; whereas many teachers nowadays hold the view that any student who has a reasonable chance of obtaining a PhD degree, should be aided – often actively pushed – to that end. This brings me to my second point: that, insofar as research can be taught or directed, many teachers themselves lack the balance of qualities which will inspire their students. They naturally require the traits listed above but in addition they need integrity, courage and a gift for getting along with young people.

Integrity is needed if they are not going to use their students simply as stooges to carry out their own pet projects, if they are publicly to give credit where credit is due and if they are to spend sufficient time working over their students' data with them and ensuring that references which conflict with the work are included. Courage is required especially when the admission must be made either that the research project is poor or that the student should never have been accepted to do research. An unfortunate student is occasionally handed on from one Supervisor to another – none having the strength of mind to tell him that he is not suited to research – until, after three or more unhappy years, he fails to gain his PhD.

Directing, or supervising, research is part of the university teacher's job. Like teaching at the undergraduate level, it is highly skilled and, once again, there is no instruction provided for it. Its case is even more parlous than that of university lecturing, since the undergraduate does at least have the opportunity of sampling a fair number of different lecturers, but the director of research will, if all went well, have had direct knowledge of only one style of supervising – that which he experienced during his own years as a research student.

In lecturing, at least the number of hours per term is stipulated and – barring illness or acts of God – the lecturer is expected to stick to this. But the number of hours per term which a supervisor gives to his research students may differ from one (or none) to a dozen or more. The same variation holds in regard to the supervisor's offering of ideas, his willingness to discuss and constructively criticize the work and the thesis. Some supervisors make themselves available during most working hours, others will meet their research students by appointment only, yet others cultivate a striking talent for elusiveness. Supervisors vary greatly also in their realization of the importance of meeting their research students socially.

Social life apart, it is suggested that a reasonable minimum of supervision hours per term should be laid down as the research student's right, that the number of such students a director accepts should not exceed an agreed maximum and that it should be easy and generally accepted for a research student to have readily available 'a second opinion', if he feels that he is not getting on well with his allotted supervisor.

The main purpose of this chapter, however, is to discuss the pros and cons of university teaching versus research from the point of view of the staff member. It is possible and desirable to combine lecturing with conducting one's own research? Or is it felt that this is an EITHER/OR choice: that limitations of time, energy and concentration do not permit a heavy lecturing load in conjunction with a continuance of one's own research?

At the risk of inducing a trance, the usual qualifications must be made: the answer will vary to some extent with the weight of the lecture-load, the relation between the two or more topics, the degree of experience of the lecturer and, above all, his temperament. He may, for instance, as he grows older, find it increasingly difficult 'to switch off and on' from one mode of thought to another. In that event he may prefer to treat the vacations as a time for research and writing, and the terms as a time for concentrating on teaching and its problems.

My own belief is that teaching and research, far from competing with each other as rivals, are almost two faces of the same coin. Not only should university teaching *involve* some research, and research *demand* to be incorporated in university teaching, but each actively improves the quality of the other. Each throws out new ideas for the other – and, without the constant infusion of new ideas, both activities become sterile.

The suggestion that teaching and research are mutually compatible is, of course, far from novel. Educationists in many fields have combined the two since the days of Socrates. What is newer (and also, evidently, very old) is the concept of student participation in lectures, partly because such open discussion provides a testing-ground for what the lecturer says. Some of his students produce criticisms of ideas, which are more or less well-accepted, but which the challenged lecturer has to rethink and substantiate. Other students may produce new ideas on the topic, not all of which should be summarily rejected. The students are young, fresh, uninvolved and unprejudiced – partly as a result of their relative ignorance and partly because they are as yet uncommitted to any one particular line of thought. Thus teaching, especially by the participation technique, can sometimes give a fillip to research.

On the other hand, his own current research can be a great help to the teacher, as such. It is absorbingly interesting (unless he is in the wrong field or the wrong job) and research varies from stage to stage, and project to project – in a way which teaching does not necessarily do. Many lecturers complain after a few years that they are bored with teaching, that they find it monotonous. This is less likely to happen if they keep their research going, for two tasks are inevitably less monotonous than one and most research is less repetitious than most teaching. Furthermore, if their research work is related to any of their lecture courses or tutorials, this very fact will make for variety, since they will wish to incorporate their results into their teaching. This of course is more exciting for the student as well as for the teacher. It has already been suggested that the lecturer should not confine himself to material which is readily available in textbooks and journals. The inclusion in lectures of his current research findings and those of his colleagues is an excellent recipe for avoiding the beaten track and keeping his teaching live and up-to-date. In particular it will furnish him with vivid unexpected examples: these may transform an otherwise dull lecture into a stimulating, memorable one – ex-students sometimes admitting in later life that a specific illustration has pleasurably stayed with them, thus enabling them to remember the general point which, they claim, would otherwise have been misunderstood or forgotten.

The approach of the research worker is, typically, 'I wonder whether . . .', 'Why does such-and-such . . .' and 'It would be fun if . . .'. His attitude is both sophisticated and childlike. The sophistication lies in his methodology, experimental design, background knowledge and the techniques for analysing and evaluating his results. But in his freshness of outlook, questioning of what is usually taken for granted, and willingness to entertain any hypothesis, he is childlike. It is no coincidence that research workers and children tend to get on so well together; nor that some of the most successful children's stories have been written by distinguished researchers-cum-teachers, such as Lewis Carroll, J. B. S. Haldane, C. S. Lewis and J. R. R. Tolkien.

On reflection, it is not difficult to see what the child and the eminent have in common. Both prefer silence to small-talk, and – in preference to either of these – they will talk about something 'real'. Both go straight *ad rem*, tacitly disdaining the benign bush-beating with which most adults start (and sometimes pursue) a conversation. Both are uncompromising, ignoring the unwritten rules as to what topics of talk or what activities are socially acceptable, and what it is admissible – because familiar or bland – to do or to say on these matters.

Most young children have these traits to begin with and lose them, more or less gradually, as they are conditioned by society. The Carrolls and the Haldanes are, in these respects, childlike (though not childish) in maturity. They either re-find these childhood qualities when they are grown-up or, occasionally, they have sufficient strength of mind to mature without ever losing these qualities of directness and curiosity and forthright observation. Other adults refer to them, with affectionate tolerance, as *enfants terribles*.*

This chapter has dealt mainly with the question of teaching and/or research for members of university staff and with the difficulties of explaining to undergraduates just what is involved in research work. In the following chapter a kind of halfway house is considered, namely, the practice of requiring undergraduates in their final year to undertake a mini research project.

---

*D. W. Winnicott goes so far as to equate *the play* of the child (or adult) with *the creative activity* of the adult (or child): chapter 4 of Ref. 21 in the bibliography of this book.

Chapter X

The undergraduate research project as a teaching device

> 'Until all teachers are geniuses and enthusiasts, nobody will learn anything, except what they teach themselves'. 'Still', said Mr Porteous, 'I wish I hadn't had to learn so much by myself. I wasted a lot of time finding out how to set to work and where to discover what I wanted.'
>
> Aldous HUXLEY

Brief essays, which range in practice from two to twenty pages, have long been requested of undergraduates at weekly or fortnightly intervals (see Chapter VII). The function of such essays is to enable the student to learn to write relevantly and vividly – or to keep him in practice, if he has already acquired this capacity – to ascertain whether he is deriving something of value from his reading and lectures, to help him to determine which aspects of his subject most appeal to him, to discover for himself what he thinks about the various aspects and to provide student-inspired material for discussion in tutorials. These essays generally cover many of the topics with which the candidate will be faced in his three-hour examination papers.

The long essay, or the mini-thesis, is something quite different and is intended to serve other ends. This device is being tried out every year in an increasing number of departments. It consists of asking the student in his final year, to select some specialized topic and to spend a certain (usually unspecified) number of hours researching on it under an agreed supervisor. Towards the end of the academic year, he is asked to hand in a report on his project.

In most departments where this practice is past the experimental stage, a small proportion of the marks in the final examination is allocated to the report by the examiners – who also devote a short time to discussing it with the candidate. This allows the latter to 'defend' his thesis (should he so desire), to explain any points which may have interested the examiners or raised their hackles and to pose, in his turn, any queries which may have arisen during the more traditional part of the examination or during the student's university course generally. The brief *viva voce* usually also carries a few marks.

This scheme is being tried in the arts, the sciences and the social sciences, including 'education'. In some cases it is compulsory, in others it is optional – students who decline to do a research project taking one or two additional examination papers. Members of staff usually offer a wide variety of research problems from which to choose, along with suggested methods of tackling them. If, however, a student offers a convincing suggestion of his own, he will usually be allowed to work on it, if a staff member with germane knowledge and interests will undertake to supervise it. In some departments students may choose to work singly or, if appropriate, in pairs. In the latter event, for purposes of examination marking, they have to write certain sections of the report separately and to indicate clearly for which parts of the work they are individually responsible.

As the chapter heading suggests, this procedure is used mainly as a teaching device. The student learns – and retains – a great deal more about an (admittedly fractional) part of his subject than even the most dedicated would ever absorb from text books and lectures alone. But it is perhaps worth noting, in passing, that even his reading may well be favourably affected where it relates to his project: he reads here like a hound on the scent, whereas a lot of his other reading is analogous rather to a puppy randomly sampling the aromas of the shrubs in an unfamiliar park.

Motivation tends to be strong in these final year researches. The student selects his own project – though if his first choice is also the first preference of several other students, he may of course have to settle for his second or third choice. He investigates and manipulates the material *he* has gathered, thus identifying with the work to an extent that is scarcely possible in other circumstances. He learns to follow up references, to read them critically, to judge which carry the most weight.

He also learns something of the other essentials of research. As suggested in the last chapter, this is a process he can understand only by doing. It is one thing to be informed in advance of the obstacles encountered by the research worker – the inconsistency of earlier scholars in the field, the frequency with which negative or inconclusive results are obtained, the recalcitrance of guinea-pigs and of apparatus-in-the-making – but it is quite another to experience them at firsthand. The student finds such hitches in turn incredible, infuriating and, finally, instructive. Their existence is also uniquely challenging. He tends to believe, at first, that only he has such an extraordinary run of bad luck and that the course of research, if well-planned, will normally run smoothly.

Graduates, however, who have been exposed to this experience claim, not uncommonly, that it was the most fulfilling aspect of their work as an undergraduate and the part which has made the most lasting impression. Occasionally they become so enthralled by what began as a mini-research problem that they wish to develop it as a full-scale, three-year project. This has been known to occur and, sometimes, to result in a fruitful piece of adult research. This is admittedly exceptional, but the teaching value of the device is the rule rather than the exception, and the innovation is being made primarily with teaching – or, rather, with learning – in mind.

Successful and popular though it tends to be, the technique inevitably has certain drawbacks. Perhaps the greatest of these is the immense variety found among the directors (or supervisors) of projects. For the student to gain the maximum benefit from his year of research, his director needs to be ingenious, conscientious and generous. Ingenuity is required to think up problems which are novel but not contrived; which are serious enough to capture the student's imagination yet which can be expected to yield results within a few months; which are sufficiently clearcut to point the student in a specific direction but are open-ended enough to enable him to implement his own ideas should any occur to him. It is sometimes needed, too, to assist the student to extract something positive from a turmoil of inconclusive findings!

Conscientiousness is required if the student is not to feel importunate or helpless. It is particularly important in these research projects that the supervisor should be available, ready at all times with his encouragement and guidance, since lack of direction at certain stages of the project may disproportionately delay its progress. The director should be conscientious, too, in his advice about ways of interpreting data, ensuring that the student understands the how and why of the methods suggested and, in the later stages, that the writing-up does justice to the work. Generosity is required in respect of the time and the praise he is willing to bestow on his student and – if the project goes well – in his public acceptance of the work as largely that of the student himself.

Students, naturally, vary greatly in the extent to which they need help. There is thus a strong element of luck in the matching of student with project-director. This is one reason why it is important to have a *viva voce*, or at least a brief discussion, between student and examiners. It enables the latter to form some opinion of the extent to which the student needed – and received – help from his supervisor, both in planning the work and in drawing conclusions from the data.

The other drawbacks are more closely related to the actual technique of the research project as a means of learning. It is sometimes thought that the projects demand too much time from the student: time that is devoted, inevitably, to some minor aspect of the discipline he is studying: time that would otherwise be spent on matters more central to his work – though the latter point is, of course, by no means certain.

Finally, many perfectly competent undergraduates are not suited to do research, on however small a scale. They may be capable of sustained reading and listening, they understand and assimilate, they discuss and write articulately. But, with such students, their attitude is one of acceptance: finding out is not for them. With such students in mind – as well as those who are generally less able – it is surely desirable to retain the optional character of the mini-thesis. Those who prefer to take an additional paper or two and forgo the joys, or hopes, of discovery should be allowed to do so. This leads to a further objection, namely, the difficulty of comparing performance on a three-hour paper with performance on a short dissertation – the latter being written in the student's own time, on a topic close to his heart and polished, if he is lucky, by his research supervisor.

The symbiosis of student and project-director has already been mentioned, in connection with the indispensability of the short oral examination. There are other advantages in having a *viva voce* in addition to written papers. The student-examiner confrontation reminds both that the other is human. Not only is this reminder salutary but the situation also offers an opportunity for a student to evince certain aspects of his intellect and personality which may have failed to come over in his written work. He may be more coherent when talking than writing; he may reveal himself as perceptive or as quick and cogent in argument; he may satisfactorily explain some section of his research report which had mystified the examiners. On the other hand, he may, of course, reveal the fact that he was himself unclear as to what he was doing in the project and that the woolliness in his report reflects a genuine confusion of thought or failure to understand. Moreover, it is not unknown for the examiners to discover when a student is defending his thesis that certain parts of it are, indeed, not 'his' at all: his vagueness may stimulate the examiners to look further into the matter, leading – on rare but unforgettable occasions – to the discovery that the candidate has inserted chunks of some obscure work into what purports to be his own.

The *viva voce* is particularly useful if the candidate is 'border-line' either between two degree classes or divisions, or between pass and fail. By tacit consent, if the candidate does well in the *viva*, this may ease him up into the higher of the two examination results. Seldom, if ever, will the oral discussion pull him down from whatever heights he would have attained on his written work alone. Further advantages of including a *viva* are that, in the rather rare cases in which examiners differ in their judgment, the student's performance in the oral may help them to reach agreement. Lastly, the student is likely to meet other interview-situations when he leaves university and applies for jobs, and he will find that practice is useful in this skill as in others.

On the other hand, there are certain drawbacks to the *viva voce*. Like all interview situations, its outcome is greatly dependent on the interaction of the personalities of the participants. This is subjective, chancy and perhaps more subject to fluctuations of mood and stress than are other methods of assessment, owing to the brevity of the *viva*, its uniqueness (one only, as opposed to several three-hour papers) and the fact that a quirk in *one* of the participants inevitably affects his relationship with all the others.

Thus, the brief oral examination has its disadvantages as well as its very marked assets. It is, however, an indispensable part of the research project, though not all students may realize at the time how essential it is.

What is it, then, that renders the research project as a teaching device rewarding and popular for the most part with undergraduates? The answer would seem to be threefold. First, many students see it as 'fairer' than the traditional three-hour paper. They feel more in command of the situation, less threatened by limitations of time and less subject to the chance factor of what particular questions are asked – a factor whose importance in examination papers they tend to over-estimate. Secondly, they enjoy its long-term character, as compared with the weekly essay or – in the case of scientists – the bi-weekly Practical. They relish the fact that *they* decide how long they are going to spend on their project, and just *when* they are going to spend this time. The more leisurely approach seems to them more in keeping with human dignity. The open-endedness of the project system, and the flexibility with respect to time, creates an experience of greater independence than they derive from the more traditional teaching devices.

Thirdly, they often appreciate the opportunity which the system offers for working alongside a member of staff – whom they might not otherwise have had the chance of getting to know. There is a mutual give-and-take in the project set-up, the student's work sometimes being valuable to his project-supervisor and the supervisor being valuable to the student. This sort of teamwork is often pleasurable as well as instructive. It has parallels in the outside world – a state for which the university student often longs or thinks he longs.

Thus the virtues of the system, from the viewpoint of the student, can perhaps be summed up in the phrase 'greater freedom of action'. There are, in fact, other advantages in the research project scheme which tend to be realized by the student only some time after he has graduated. One is the fact that even negative results may be instructive. The student is delighted if he obtains positive results, that is, results which confirm his hypothesis – whether literary, scientific or social – and he tends at first to be very disappointed if his findings conflict with the suppositions which prompted the project. He may gradually learn, however, that such conflicting results are not without interest; indeed, on occasion, they have more far-reaching significance than do straightforward positive results, wholly compatible with all that preceded the experiment. He learns too in practice – what has hitherto been only an academic point – that, whilst results can refute a position, they cannot irrevocably establish it.

When writing up his project, the student also learns something of the inseparability of subject-matter and presentation. This is a hard and a useful lesson. Informing someone of this fact is pretty ineffectual: witness about half the papers submitted to Journals. But when the student realizes that his supervisor simply cannot understand parts of his report – that this is because the supervisor is less familiar with the material than is the writer, and that the examiners will be still less familiar – then the student may learn the virtues of clear exposition. He may learn also that, contrary to his schooldays impression of 'the longer the better', it is the case that 'the shorter the better' – providing nothing important is omitted.

Finally, a word about the research project from the viewpoint of the examiner. Although the reading of the reports and the holding of *vivas* is time-consuming, most examiners will opt for these rather than for reading a further set of examination scripts. The latter is an enervating task, often tedious and almost always done under great pressure. The research projects, however, often prove stimulating, they are pleasantly varied and they can usually be assessed at a less breathless pace than can the scripts. Any procedure which helps to keep examiners sane and cheerful should surely be welcomed.

Chapter XI

Is graduate research teachable?

'We often discover what *will* do, by finding out what will not do; and probably he who never made a mistake never made a discovery.' Samuel SMILES

It would perhaps be pretentious to describe my recent inquiries into graduate research work as itself a piece of research – although there are definite similarities. I had certain clearly formulated questions. These were along the following lines: What is the hallmark of research and, especially, of effective research? Which comes first, the research problem or the research student? How is his supervisor selected? And how, in due course, are his examiners selected? Does he necessarily work towards a higher degree? And, if so, at what stage is the level of degree determined? What are the requisite qualifications for the successful research student? Should any graduate who could probably achieve a PhD be urged to embark on such a course? Or should such graduates, on the contrary, be positively discouraged, in order to test the extent of their drive and staying-power – two qualities which are very necessary in research.

My aims were to answer these questions. My motivation, both intrinsic and extrinsic, was strong. I wished to discover the answers for their own sake and also to produce an informative chapter. Thus far, the analogy with genuine research would appear to hold. But the *methods* here are different, since I did not carry out any experiments; nor did I have any hypotheses, to be confirmed or refuted. Moreover the chapter is more discursive, less conclusive and very much shorter than is the final section of a typical dissertation.

Perhaps the best method of finding out what makes for a good research student or for productive research teaching is to examine the more frequent complaints made, first by graduate students and secondly by supervisors (or directors) of research. A complaint often made by research students concerns the non-availability of their supervisor. I would not go as far as Mrs Gold, a scientist who has told me that she likes to have her research students actually working in her room in the laboratory, 'in order that the whole idea of research should permeate them, that they should pick up the technique and learn what research is all about.'

Whilst this may work well with Mrs Gold, many students (and supervisors) would find it inhibiting and stultifying. The research student should experience some measure of independence – in his work, his reading, his hours, his discussions with others – and, in order to acquire this, he needs either a room of his own or, if accommodation is in short supply, a room shared with one or two fellow research students.

Many young research workers, however, suffer from difficulties of the opposite kind. They are accepted by a staff member – who is an authority in the relevant field – but who neither offers a set time for regular discussions at weekly or fortnightly intervals, nor welcomes informal visits from his research students whenever they feel inclined. There are some supervisors who indeed claim to operate on this basis, saying that a regular meeting time is too formal and 'there may be nothing to talk about' but who are, in practice, unavailable when the student calls. He is met with a PLEASE DO NOT ENTER notice on the door, or a secretary who explains that Dr Garnet is at a meeting – or he may just learn from the grapevine that 'Garnet is broadcasting again'.

This is discouraging for young Kingfisher who has tried twice in the previous week to contact Dr Garnet, since he wants to discuss some results, he needs a consultation before embarking on the next stage of his research, and he begins to feel (as several such students have put it to me) that 'the research student is the lowest form of life'. It may be that Garnet is over-burdened with administrative commitments, or is engrossed in his own research, or is pathologically shy. Academics are prone to be overwhelmed by one or more of these ailments (I know of one, now deceased, who more than once took refuge in a cupboard, at the approach of a visitor!) But in this event, they should drastically curtail the number of research students whom they undertake to supervise, and carefully vet those whom they accept, for determination and independence of spirit.

At the other extreme may be met the supervisor who will not allow his research students even minimal freedom. This is a much rarer phenomenon and it is likely to be confined to rather young supervisors who have very few research students. The novice in research should be allowed to make a few mistakes. He should not be kept on too tight a rein and if, after discussion, he wishes to try out an idea which the supervisor thinks misguided, he should be allowed to do so provided that this will not involve an inordinate amount of time which may well prove to be wasted. Such latitude is desirable, partly because trial and error is an essential part of research. Moreover, the student may well think resentfully that it would have been a worthwhile idea, if only he had been allowed to follow it up; and it is, of course, not unknown, in such cases, for the supervisor to be mistaken and the idea indeed to prove fruitful.

The supervisor should, then, be available for discussion with his research student but should not be perpetually breathing down his neck. Related to this question is that of the degree of interest which the supervisor has in the research topic. If he lacks interest and has taken on the student because nobody else in the Department would do so, or because he believes that his academic status depends largely upon the number of research students he directs, Kingfisher may well be in for a bad time. He will soon become aware of Garnet's lack of enthusiasm for the project and, unless he is exceptionally strong-minded – or fortunate in finding some unofficial supervisor – a great deal of his own initial fervour may evaporate. On the other hand it can be equally discouraging to find oneself, as a research student, a kind of cog in one's supervisor's favourite machine, taken on to do a particular project because Garnet passionately wants it done and lacks the time to do it himself. The research student must be encouraged to identify himself with his research project, and this demands the right amount of support. 'The right amount' is somewhat question-begging; it varies, of course, with the ability and self-confidence of the research student.

Naturally, some students want more help and encouragement than others. It is here that the supervisor needs to be adaptable, becoming aware that whereas Kingfisher may require spoon-feeding to a certain extent, Umber thrives on being left largely on his own. And since some otherwise good supervisors lack this sort of adaptability, it is sometimes the task of the Head of Department to allocate certain types of research student to certain types of supervisor. He should take into account personalities as well as topics.

Something that does *not* vary with individuals is the importance of the intrinsic merit of the research project. It must be worthwhile and be seen to be so by both the student and his supervisor. It is not unknown, especially in the arts, for a topic to be selected simply because it has not been chosen before – and, all too often, the reason for its not having been chosen earlier becomes apparent. Furthermore, the alleged reason is not a genuine reason: it is analogous to the futility of saying that the reason for climbing Everest (or any other mountain) is 'because it is there': such a reply confuses the necessary with the sufficient. It obviously could not be climbed if it were *not* there but its mere existence does not constitute the reason for climbing it.

An ill-chosen choice of topic is less likely to occur in the domain of the natural sciences, which is expanding at an accelerating rate – though even here certain projects are not wholly suited to the novice in research. Some projects are too slight: these are unlikely to last the mandatory three years and to yield a sufficiently substantial dissertation. Some, on the other hand, are too ambitious for completion within the time allowed. The recognition of a good project demands considerable sagacity. Thus, from the very beginning the judgment of the research director is called into play.

Above all, a particular project may not suit the individual concerned. Often the research student himself will have some idea of his field of interest and sometimes he may even outline his aims and methodology in detail. When these are thought practicable by a senior member of his department this is excellent and augers well for a happy and productive partnership. Even in such ideal circumstances, however, the student should be warned of the inevitable setbacks encountered in research: the unpredictable delays, the negative instances (which may, however, prove instructive), the fact that the conduct and writing up of research requires endless checking and rechecking and, hence, that the process of actually writing the thesis is likely to take far longer than is envisaged.

It is not always easy for the examiners to tell whether an unsatisfactory thesis is so because: the problem was unsuitable (in other hands, it might have thrived); the supervisor was inefficient, uncongenial or too frequently absent; the research work was competently planned and carried out but was so poorly presented in the vital, final stage that its potential worth was obscured; or whether the student lacked the necessary intellectual ability – and had not, in this instance, been 'carried' (as sometimes happens) by his supervisor.

A brilliantly successful undergraduate does not necessarily make a good research worker (any more than he necessarily makes a good teacher). He should be academically gifted certainly but he needs also acute curiosity, attention to detail, scrupulous integrity, long-term perseverance and a burning interest in his field which consumes the various frustrations encountered. (It is one of the supervisor's tasks to distinguish between 'long-term perseverance' and mulish obstinacy.) Some departmental heads are so impressed with the need for these characteristics that they incline to underestimate the purely intellectual quality demanded.

Professor Liam Hudson claims, for instance, that students who gain Lower seconds or Third classes in their final examination are as successful in scientific research as those who obtain Upper seconds and firsts (see Ref. 8 in bibliography). His generalization from this finding is based on a misconception. Hudson fails to take into account that it is in practice very difficult for a graduate with a low degree class to gain support as a research student. Thus his teacher(s) – if they wish to secure a research grant for him – regard him as a highly exceptional individual and have to make a case proving that his university examination results altogether failed to do him justice. Whilst agreeing that the correlation between degree class and academic ability is far from 100 per cent, I do nonetheless deny that such a strong case could be made for *the majority* of lower seconds and thirds.

If the student has carried out a research project while he was an undergraduate (see Chapter X), his showing on this may prove helpful in estimating his subsequent research potential. He will probably be willing to allow his future supervisor to read his mini-thesis; and it should be possible to get a reference from the staff member who directed his undergraduate research project. These two data, supplemented, of course, by discussion with the student should enable one to decide whether his interest in research is long-term and positive (i.e. not just a way of staving off a major decision for another three years). The matter is infinitely more difficult when the potential research student is overseas, since the personalities involved may be unknown, the standards may be different, and interviewing – *before* the decision is taken – may be impracticable.

Let us assume, however, that Cherry got his first degree in Britain, that he gained a higher second class, has secured his research grant and during his first few months is performing adequately. Two further points now demand consideration: first is the question whether Cherry's supervisor, Blaze, is satisfied with the progress of his research and secondly – if the candidate stays the course – the question of examiner-selection.

The two questions are not always as simple to deal with as would appear at first sight and they may give rise to grave problems if not wisely dealt with. That some graduates get accepted for research who are not in fact suited for it is perhaps inevitable. But it is *not* inevitable that such research students should linger on, term after term, feeling increasingly miserable, producing less and less satisfactory work – until they finally turn in a poor dissertation on which they are either failed or awarded a degree lower than that for which they were originally registered.

All universities request a formal report from research directors on each of their research students once a year, and sometimes more frequently. This is not, or should not be treated as, a mere formality. If Blaze has serious doubts about Cherry's work, he should admit this in his official reports and should discuss the matter with Cherry. He should not, as quite often happens, lull himself and his student into a false sense of security along the lines that 'the start is always the hardest part', 'this is a tricky project', 'perhaps he'd do better with Sapphire' or 'you can't really judge until the work is finished' – by which time the damage done may be irreparable.

I have known more than one case in which the supervisor lacked the resolution to tell his student (and his University Board of Graduate Studies) that the student was not up to research. In such cases, in the mistaken belief that he is being kind, Blaze either does a great deal of Cherry's work for him, probably inviting disaster for Cherry at his *viva voce*, or he passes Cherry on to another supervisor, say, Sapphire, who very likely transfers him within the year to Agate – who in turn passes him on to Olive. In the worst case of this kind that I have met, the student had worked with five different supervisors in as many years! None of them had told him that he could not make the grade and when I (as external examiner, knowing nothing of this) finally met him at the *viva*, with his internal examiner, we both felt quite unable to award the degree for which he was a candidate. It seems appalling that weakness, masquerading as benevolence, should condemn a student so depressingly to waste so much of his time.

There is another situation, equally regrettable, that obtains in universities where the internal examiner is also the student's supervisor. This seems to be an indefensible system. True, when the project is worthwhile, the dissertation good, the two examiners can reach the conclusion to award the desired research degree, without too much distress on either side (though in effect one of them is not fulfilling the role of examiner at all). But when the dissertation is inadequate, the defects of the procedure are glaring.

It is a *sine qua non* of examiners that they should be impartial and approach their task without any preconceived ideas. This is clearly impossible when Blaze, in the role of supervisor, has worked closely with the candidate on his project for several years and has already been through his thesis with him. He cannot be objective in this situation. Moreover, if he has done his stuff as a supervisor, he has already said all that he thinks necessary, before the examination; and the candidate, knowing his views, will either have amended his thesis or stated his reasons for differing from Blaze – in his role of supervisor.

Thus Blaze's mind is already made up, before the *viva voce* examination: if he thought that Cherry and his thesis were not up to the standard of a DPhil (or whatever degree Cherry is attempting) he would presumably not put himself in the false position of examining him for it. Yet Blaze *is* in a false position in the sense of trying to perform two mutually incompatible functions simultaneously. He has the unenviable choice of either remaining silent throughout the *viva* – thus leaving the whole burden on the shoulders of Ginger, the external examiner – or of raising only trivial or far-fetched issues, which had not been worth raising at a time when Cherry could have dealt with them.

In fact, as Ginger becomes uncomfortably aware, it is Blaze, rather than Cherry, whom Ginger is effectively examining, with reference both to the thesis and the oral. This can be disconcerting for both the examiners and deeply distressing for Cherry, the candidate – who is completely hamstrung. He can neither say: 'Oh that was Dr. Blaze's idea' nor can he call on Blaze in his capacity as supervisor, since Blaze is wearing his other hat.

The custom of having at least two examiners is an excellent one, but there must be two (or more) independent minds at work, in practice as well as in theory. They need to come fresh to the thesis and the candidate, without any preconceived ideas or personal loyalties.

It is, admittedly, not always easy to find two examiners, one from the same university and one from elsewhere, both of whom are authorities in the arcane realm which Cherry has made his own. Indeed, it sometimes happens that by the time he has followed up all the references, enjoyed innumerable arguments with his fellow research students, written and discussed his thesis with Blaze, that Cherry himself is the greatest expert in the field! This does not matter and it is, in any case, not for this reason that certain universities adhere to the deplorable practice described above. It is a matter of tradition – and not even very old tradition. Two intelligent, open-minded people (and examiners lacking these traits should not be appointed), interested and well-versed in Cherry's general field will be able to assess his dissertation and his defence of it far better than can somebody personally involved in the work. Indeed, one of the best ways of discovering how well a student understands his work is to ask, frankly, for elucidation on certain points. This kind of question comes easily from the examiner who knows the background of the work but is unfamiliar with the detailed, very recent, relevant research and who is prepared to admit his relative ignorance. He will learn far more about the candidate's ability and informed interests in this way than if he adopts an attitude of omniscient superiority – whether justified or unjustified.

We are now in a position to reconsider some of the questions posed at the beginning of the chapter. The hallmark of effective research is that it should produce results, within a finite period. Negative results are sometimes as useful as positive results, though the young research worker may find them less rewarding. The choice of the word 'useful' may be queried since I do not wish to imply necessarily results of immediate practical import. This is partly because I believe that theory and practice are inextricably interwoven (see Chapter IX); and partly because theoretical findings do seem to me of great interest and value in their own right – in those cases in which no practical consequences have (as yet) emerged. The major aim of research is to advance knowledge – whether in the form of discovering facts, propounding new theories or developing the ideas of earlier workers in the field. It is desirable that the results be expressed in a form which is intelligible to those working in similar, or closely related, areas.

As to the hen-and-egg question of the research problem and the research student no clearcut answer can be given. Sometimes the one presents itself first and sometimes the other: the vital thing is that they should be well-matched. This suggests that the matching should not be done in a hurry. In fact, a preliminary exploratory period of a few months should perhaps be the rule rather than the exception, save for those cases – such as an undergraduate research project or a long-held specific ambition – where suitability of topic is abundantly clear.

The selection of supervisor and, eventually, of examiners has been discussed at length. As to the level of research degree to be aimed for: if the student appears unlikely to attain the standard of a doctorate, it is better for him to aim for a lower degree (such as MLit or MSc) than for him to be awarded such a degree and to feel that this award spells failure.

In general, graduates should not be pushed or persuaded into research work. They should be very keen as well as very able and, if they are to do well in research, they should manifest a certain tenacity in the face of opposition. Thus a balanced account – of the snags as well as the joys – of research should be given them, before they embark on it. To the extent that research, like teaching, is best learned by doing it, it cannot be taught *in toto*. Yet I obviously believe that some instruction in university teaching is desirable, otherwise I should not have written this book. The teaching of research, however, is largely done by exemplification, discussion and criticism of points of methodology and exposition. There is perhaps only one feature common to all research students whatever their subject, namely that their dissertation takes far longer to write than they anticipate, and that before it has reached an acceptable form they are ineffably bored with it! On this point, at least, the supervisor can give warning in advance and offer support towards the end.

Chapter XII

The Seminar

> 'Discussion in class, which means letting twenty young blockheads and two cocky neurotics discuss something that neither their teachers nor they know.'
>
> Vladimir NABOKOV

The seminar (or small discussion-class) differs, on the one hand, from the lecture and, on the other, from the tutorial discussed in Chapter VII. It is desirable for the student to experience at least two of these three types of instruction since one method is likely to suit some people, and a different method may make more appeal to others. Moreover, each of the three techniques has its own advantages and its pitfalls, and certain university teachers may excel at, and prefer to use, one particular type of teaching method. Ideally, the student will encounter all three while at university. The seminar is, perhaps, especially valuable in the arts and the social sciences, where learning to develop a point of view and to interact with others are essential to the discipline. On occasions, however, it can also serve a useful function in the natural sciences – and even in mathematics, where the wheels of communication sometimes need a little oiling. In the abstract realm of advanced mathematics the seminar may provide an ideal opportunity for the students to air difficulties which may not otherwise be admitted or even recognized.

'Small class' denotes roughly 8–12 students and one teacher or 'leader'. I say 'roughly' because if the numbers shrink to six or rise to 15, I should still designate this as 'seminar teaching'; and in certain cases two teachers are present. When this occurs, they must resist the temptation jointly to dominate the conversation. This can easily happen and it intimidates the shy, infuriates the eloquent and fosters the laziness or apathy of the passive.

The technique of the seminar differs from others in more important respects than mere numbers but the differences do stem mainly from the size of the group. In the tutorial, the conversation is generally based on the essay or notes produced by the student(s), and the tutor usually does a good deal of the talking. The subject matter tends to revolve around the topic of the essay, though it may extend to subjects of marginal relevance or even to general or personal matters which the student feels he needs to discuss.

In the lecture, on the other hand, the teacher will try to limit public discussion to matters strictly pertinent to the particular session – that is, if he follows the suggestions made in earlier chapters and does encourage his listeners to make contributions. It is as essential for the lecturer to eschew red herrings as it is for the chairman of a committee. All groups, whatever their size, contain members lacking in modesty and sense of relevance. If such members are not tactfully restrained, others become impatient and inevitably some vital issues have to be dealt with hurriedly or even omitted.

The seminar lies between the tutorial and the lecture, not only with regard to numbers but also in respect of leadership; of the extent to which group members get to know one another during the session; of the amount of undivided attention that the teacher gives to each member of the class; and of the degree of activity required of the students – between seminars as well as during them. Let us consider these in turn.

Seminars may take many forms. There is the so-called leaderless group – sometimes planned, specifically, to allow one or more leaders to emerge from within the group. Such aims will not be considered here since they are not concerned primarily with *teaching* – though observation of such a group in action may be extremely instructive as to the dynamics of group leadership, the importance of timing and the role of silences.

Some leaderless groups, however, are so designated simply because no senior member is present. The group may organize itself, of its own accord or under the aegis of a teacher – who, having helped to establish the group, takes little or no further part in its proceedings. Such a group consisting entirely of students, will very likely elect from its ranks a leader – or, possibly, choose a different leader each week – since it soon becomes apparent that a genuinely leaderless group behaves more like a small mob or a collection of cliques than the working party that its members desire. Without an accepted leader or chairman, several are liable to talk at the same time – with the result that little can be heard.

Alternatively, people may take to speaking in low voices to their neighbours and useful information or discussion may be lost for the majority.

This phenomenon is not confined to students: it tends to happen in all groups that are too big for the conversation naturally to remain unitary, that is, bigger than about four or five people. Nor are students the only people who need to discover for themselves that anarchy, on any scale, is the antithesis of freedom.

In seminar-teaching the function of the leader is more often taken by a member of staff. Whoever takes it, the role is an important one, on which the success of the seminar largely depends. It is highly skilled because it is not closely or rigidly defined and because one of the conditions is to ensure that everyone in the group gets something out of it – and also puts something into it. The latter is almost a prerequisite of the former.

The leader is in the group but not of it; he has to retain enough authority to ensure that only one member talks at a time yet he usually wishes the group to remain informal and unstructured. He wants to keep everybody interested yet his group may contain very varied elements, seeking different sorts of satisfaction from the course. Some may want hard information, some may be seeking confirmation of their own views, yet others may want to discover what they think by taking part in active discussion.

Thus his task is essentially to maintain balance among the group members; to elicit contributions from the silent, without artificiality, and to discourage the voluble from hogging the field, without giving offence. This problem rarely arises in lectures – where it is clear that only a small minority will be able to have a say; nor in tutorials – where the student expects to play an active part since he is required to defend, and expatiate upon, his own written work.

In general, the students taking part in a seminar will be drawn from the same year; and they will be to some extent self-selected in that they volunteer to join the group. Others may be invited to participate, but any form of coercion is likely to prove self-defeating.

The teacher will probably have personally to lead the discussion at the beginning of the course when his students are, perhaps, but little acquainted with the main theme, with him and with one another. After the first few seminars, however, he may be able to leave it more and more to the students, acting rather as a referee in a game – now tossing the ball to Miss Magenta to kick off, now retrieving it from Mr Jade

who has been dribbling for too long, now passing it to the diffident
Mr Puce to score the goal which is at this point wide open.

Many seminars are run on the system whereby a number of topics are
chosen in the first session, all related to a central theme, and each student
is asked to select one of the topics for himself. It is his task to read
around the subject, making his own bibliography, and each student in
turn will open a seminar by giving a brief talk, or reading a short paper,
in his chosen area. This should take, say, 20–25 minutes, leaving the
rest of the session for discussion of what he has said. At the end of the
course, the teacher may incorporate the various threads into one skein –
comprising multifarious weights and colours.

This system confers many benefits. It inspires each student to work
on his own, on a subject of his choice. He is motivated to follow up cases
and to pursue references which may not always be to hand; to study
something in depth and to present it in an intelligible, interesting and
concise form; to respect his deadline, for even if he is not fully prepared
when his turn comes, he knows that the whole group is depending
on him and that the show must go on. He knows, too, that he will be
judged by his peers and this is less daunting than being assessed by a
senior member. Some students are more willing to learn from one
another than from someone in authority. They find it easier to take
criticism from their fellow students – and they also gain more pleasure
from being praised by them.

For the listeners each week, too, this type of seminar may be rewarding. They learn a good deal from the research done by fellow-students on
each particular topic and, almost equally instructive, they learn from the
misunderstandings of others and their mistakes – whether of presentation or of content. The listeners have the double interest of hearing what
old Greene has to say ('old Greene' being very likely some thirty years
younger than Professor Vermillion, who is in charge of the course) and
of knowing Greene personally. By the end of a term of seminars,
many friendships will have been made, often based on mutual intellectual interests. The listeners, again, are more willing to judge the
value of the opening talk, and to express their criticisms articulately and
publicly, if the talk is given by one of their peers. It is quite an important
part of higher education to learn to make and substantiate criticisms
and to learn to accept analysis of one's own work.

By the end of the term, if all has gone well, every student will have
given at least one opening talk; most will have had some experience of
contributing to general discussion; and all will have had occasion to

read in depth and to reflect on the central theme. Ideally, the opening papers – which may well appear disconnected towards the beginning, in view of their differing headings and approaches – gradually achieve some unity towards the end of the course. If this has not occurred, the teacher may once again take an active role and attempt to reconcile the various papers or to demonstrate the legitimacy of agreeing to differ. If all goes well, those students who possess originality will have learned also something of the art of creative thinking – of learning which hunches to trust and how to express them convincingly – in addition to the skills of assimilating and criticizing.

It remains to say something of the physical conditions of the seminar since these, again, differ widely from those of the lecture and the tutorial. There is of course no need for visual aids or a microphone since the seminar usually takes place in an ordinary room, with comfortable space for the 8–12 students and their teacher. Acoustics, then, present no problem. But it is worth considering the questions of seating, lighting and timing.

The chairs are best arranged in a circle or around a table. The virtues of this are that everybody can see everyone else's face; no 'we and they' feeling is generated; and there is no suggestion of a hierarchical seating arrangement. If two (or more) teachers are present, it is best if they do not sit next to one another – partly to avoid any insinuation of authoritarian solidarity and partly to discourage their talking directly to one another, short-circuiting the students. If there are any particularly enviable positions (such as sitting near a radiator in the Winter) or unattractive positions (such as having the sun in one's eyes) these will be determined on a first come, first served basis.

If the room is lighted by electricity, care should be taken to ensure that it is sufficiently bright and evenly distributed for everyone to make notes who wishes to do so, and nowhere so dazzling that discomfort may be caused. The venue should not be immediately above or below a music room and should not be within close earshot of noisy traffic or motorcycles starting up – or children (or students) at play.

The duration of a seminar is often longer than the statutory hour of the lecture. It may be predetermined for, say, an hour and a half or even 2–$2\frac{1}{2}$ hours. (More than two and a half hours is, in my opinion, definitely too long.) Or the length may be resolved by the participants, at the first meeting. In any case a set time should be agreed and should be maintained, within reasonable limits, however gripping the discussion may be as the seminar draws to a close. The tendency for the most rewarding talk to occur towards the end of the session will persist, whatever the length of time allowed; and students (and teacher) like to know in advance when they will be free to leave – without feeling that they are disrupting the group or behaving discourteously. Individuals will probably continue to chat with one another as they leave the room.

If the seminar is arranged to last longer than one and a half-hours, it is a good idea to organize coffee or tea – or even beer or sherry – if time and place permit. This may occur during the seminar, causing little interruption, or it may be planned as a short interval, perhaps halfway through the session. The background music provided by certain seminar leaders is, however, to be avoided!

To sum up: the seminar type of teaching may take one of several forms but its basic aim is always to produce open discussion which is both informal and centralised. The task of the leader – whether student or lecturer – is to ensure that the talk retains its spontaneity and informality without losing its relevance to the main theme; that every participant makes some active contribution; and that the members of the group feel pleasurably 'stretched' by the end of each seminar. On the negative side, he must beware of the formation of little cliques and of the tendency to refer all questions back to him.

Indeed his task may be likened in some respects to that of a host giving a dinner party of about a dozen people. There are certain obvious differences, such as the absence of a central theme at a party, the lack of necessity to keep people to the point and the delight of hearing several animated conversations going on at the same time. Yet the similarities are many: the host is in a position to dominate the conversation but he should not wish to do so; he must be able to relieve silences and potential embarrassment without obvious subterfuge; and his aim is to enable his guests to feel both relaxed and stimulated. In both situations the success of the venture depends largely on the constitution of the group, the congeniality of the venue and the manner of the convenor. But, whereas an unsuccessful dinner party is irretrievable once it is over, there is always hope that the next seminar will go better – until the end of the term is reached.

Chapter XIII

What is successful teaching?

> He was more an attorney than philosopher, and he lacked
> that sublime humility which is the crown of genius. For
> this obstinate persuasion that he alone knew the mind of
> God, that he alone could interpret the designs of the
> Creator, what did it result from if not from a congenital
> lack of higher modesty which replies 'I do not know'. . . ?
>
> Edmund GOSSE

The rationale of this book is that university teaching is a skill which
can be acquired, to some extent, by receiving instruction. It is not
suggested that instruction can or should replace experience in the field
but that the beginner will be helped to attain competence faster and at a
higher level, if he considers the sort of points raised in these pages than if
he gives his early lecture courses merely by the light of nature and of his
own experience of student days. It is suggested, too, that such consideration would involve less wasted time on his part and less wear and tear on
the part of his pupils than is at present the case.

If this hypothesis is to be verified, some definition of 'success' in
teaching is needed and also some criteria by which to evaluate the
degree of success achieved by any given lecture course or lecturer. In
accordance with earlier suggestions, some of the attributes of a successful
course are taken to be active enjoyment on the part of the students, a
feeling that they are being intellectually 'stretched', awareness of
stimulation such as leads them to pursue further the topic and others
germane to it – and these imply at least a minimum of *understanding*
on their part. It is suggested too that a mode of teaching which evokes
constructive criticism may well be more valuable than one which
assumes unreflecting acceptance.

There are three ways in which reactions to teaching can be assessed:
(a) feedback, direct from the students, (b) self-appraisal by the teacher,
(c) external assessment, for example, by means of academic examinations
and judgments of colleagues. These are not mutually exclusive but each
has its own merits, and it is highly desirable for the novice – and, indeed,
the experienced lecturer – to make use of all these means, where this is
feasible.

Student feedback may be solicited or unsolicited. The most obvious
unsolicited feedback is of the number attending the classes throughout
the term. Whilst it would be an oversimplification to say, in Orwellian
fashion, 'more means good; less means bad', it is probably true that ever-
decreasing attendance at a particular course of lectures is not a healthy
sign. The phenomenon can and should be used constructively, however,
as a basis for investigation: Why are the numbers dropping? Why have
you stopped attending? And *you*? Are the lectures considered too
difficult? – too easy? Does the lecturer go too fast? – too slowly? Can
he not be easily heard? Is he heard but not understood? Is he tedious
to listen to? Can it all be readily found in the textbooks? . . .

Students are usually ready to answer such questions and also to add
further comments of their own, provided that these can be offered
anonymously. This brings us to 'solicited feedback'. It is a good idea to
ask the students for their views on their lecturers – and not only in those
courses which are ill-attended. Indeed, routine annual assessment by the
students on each of their courses would appear to be highly desirable.
This is best done by means of a rating sheet covering such questions as
are raised in the preceding paragraph. A five-point scale is preferable
to a Yes/No form of questionnaire, since it yields more information –
both on the lecture course and the individual making the assessments –
and it does not oversimplify complex issues to the same extent as does a
simple affirmative/negative.

Space should be left on the sheet for additional comments. These may
be useful when drawing up the subsequent year's rating sheet and they
will occasionally shed light on some aspect of lecturing whose importance had been overlooked. It is unlikely that every student on the
course will respond to the invitation, but efforts should be made to enlist
the co-operation of as many as possible. If only 50 per cent, or less, of
the members of the course take part, it is likely that the respondents
will be unrepresentative of the class as a whole.

Naturally enough, some lecturers are not keen on such a procedure.
Their rationalizations are sometimes very interesting. 'How can the

students know what's good for them?' and 'Only an expert in the field can assess a lecture course' are two frequent reactions. The former remark illustrates a lordly attitude, which the contemporary student does not tolerate. He takes the understandable view that it is the students themselves who know best what they want and need; and whilst admitting that the university teacher's knowledge of the subject exceeds that of the pupils, he is aware that in every class there are some individuals with a potential equal to, or greater than, that of the teacher. My own opinion is that some students are in fact mistaken about their needs; and their wants are often ephemeral and contradictory. But I strongly believe that they should be given the opportunity of expressing their wishes and also that these are sometimes highly instructive.

The second comment – that only an expert can judge the value of a course – is a half-truth. A non-expert is unlikely to create a wholly satisfactory lecture course. But it is no use producing a scholarly exposé of the subject which, whilst acceptable to a colleague, conveys little meaning to the non-expert. Undergraduate lecture-courses are not *intended* for specialists in the field.

A somewhat subtler rationalization may take the form: 'But such a questionnaire would provide a perfect opportunity for leg-pulling: how can we possibly know whether the students are taking it seriously?' It is difficult to think of any form of human communication which is not open to this particular danger; and if one is prepared to teach intelligent and articulate young adults, one must also be prepared to take certain risks.

The lecturer who wishes to forgo the opportunity of gaining feedback on his course rarely, if ever, says 'I'm sure I'm doing a good job and, if I'm not, I don't want to know about it' or 'I know I'm an indifferent lecturer and it will do no good to have this confirmed by the students' or 'the course is fine but there's something odd about the students this year'. Yet these surely are the messages he conveys by his transparent rationalizations. One has only to recall the furore aroused by Aubrey Jones's suggestion* that students as customers, should express their opinions about the efficacy of their lecturers, and that these opinions should be taken into account as part-determinants of each lecturer's salary-scale, to realize the extreme vulnerability of many university teachers. Vulnerability begets defensive, aggressive and rigid reactions; these are often incompatible with a learning attitude; and a learning attitude is surely appropriate to the teacher, no less than to his pupil.

---

*Standing Reference on the Pay of University Teachers in Great Britain. Reprinted 1969. NBPI rept. No. 98, HMSO.

Questionnaires and attendance figures are not the only available methods of feedback. Further clues may be found in the extent to which those who do attend doze or chat to one another during the lecture, or knit or read the newspaper. An excellent, more positive, indicator is the number and enthusiasm of students who crowd round the dais at the end of the hour eagerly requesting references or elucidation of some point, or even free-associating to some of the ideas considered in the course of the lecture.

Such clues overlap with what was described above as 'self-appraisal by the teacher'. If the lecturer himself has a clear idea of the effects he wishes to produce, he can infer a good deal from the kind of evidence adumbrated in the previous paragraph. If he sees his function purely as that of informant – as dispensing facts and figures, for the students to take down in their note books and subsequently memorize – then he will presumably not welcome a flood of questions at the end of the lecture. He may elect to avoid close contact with his pupils, preferring to remain aloof, perhaps slipping out of the lecture hall as soon as he has cast his last pearl. He will thus effectively protect himself from self-appraisal – whether it be discomfiting or reassuring. He considers that his job is done when he has delivered his informative, impersonal lecture.

If, however, he welcomes the human contact, he likes to discover which topics most interest the contemporary student and he believes that such discovery may increase his effectiveness as a teacher, then he will not see these questions as importunate but as appreciative expressions of interest and commitment and, given this viewpoint, he will not grudge his pupils a little extra time.

For the lecturer who believes that public discussion is more intellectually challenging and more conducive to understanding, than is a public monologue, the best means of self-appraisal is in the frequency and liveliness of the contributions elicited from his audience. Such a teacher will begin his first session by inviting participation; he makes it clear that any questions or comments which are relevant will be in order; and, when the first contribution is made, he clearly welcomes it – by evincing pleasure and interest and, above all, by treating the questioner with respect. He may need to remind his students of their privilege at the beginning of his second session. But after this, if he has used the technique skilfully, there will be no dearth of queries throughout the course.

Lack of participation in such a lecture course is to be regarded as a failure on his part. It may result from apathy and listlessness. His students may appear uninterested because he is not covering what they had hoped for (inappropriate handout). Or the apathy may be due to his lecturing 'on the wrong wave-length' (so rarefied that it proves unassimilable or so simple that it is unstimulating). Faulty 'pitching' here is part of a vicious circle since it is precisely by means of participation that the lecturer can ascertain whether he is indeed on the right wave-length – and, if he is not, how to improve matters.

On the other hand, inadequate participation may stem from the lecturer's manner: although he claims to welcome comments, the message reaching his audience may be that he prefers to read aloud from his lecture notes, uninterruptedly, in the pre-arranged order, secure in the knowledge that nothing need be omitted. This message may be confirmed by the way in which he deals with the few tentative questions offered by the students who have the temerity to take him at his word. 'I thought I had already made that clear', 'This is outside my terms of reference', 'I'm coming to that shortly', 'That point is fully dealt with in the second reference on the board' . . . a few such replies, early on in the course, will reduce the vast majority of his listeners to silence.

The resulting *jejune* participation should also be regarded as a failure, even though it be due largely to the lecturer's – perhaps unconscious – choice. The teacher who genuinely desires public discussion, as opposed to a monologue will, after a little practice, usually succeed in arousing it. The disciplines for which this approach is unsuitable seem to me few, but they probably exist. Excepting these, however, participation is a useful means of self-appraisal for the teacher, in addition to being a valuable teaching device. If comments and questions come thick and fast, if they are pertinent to the main trend of the course and if many members of the class participate, this indicates that education is taking place in an important sense. Whether it is more crucial educationally that the teacher should reach the end of his notes, or that the students should be stimulated into taking an active part, during and after the lecture, is a moot point.

External assessment of any given course may be made by colleagues and also by means of essays and examination answers on germane subjects. The judgment of colleagues is usually rather indirect. They, like the teacher himself, observe whether the numbers attending are liable to rise, fall or remain constant, throughout the course and from year to year. They tend not to request informal criticism or appreciation from the students but they are bound to perceive attitudes and to make inferences in the course of their dealings with individual students, in their role of tutor or supervisor or director of studies. Occasionally a student will seek help, in distress because he feels he is gaining nothing from a particular course; less frequently, a student will take the trouble to express appreciation of a certain course.

Unrepresentative and haphazard though these straws may be, they do give some indication of the direction of the wind, and the teacher who fails to respond to such indicators is apt to be head-in-sand – an uncomfortable position in which to lecture. Most enlightening (and at times most horrifying) are the external criteria which a teacher can scarcely fail to recognize, and should find difficult to rationalize, in the form of students' essays and examination answers, patently based on his own lectures.

It is an all too common experience to come upon a passage written by a student – a passage which combines an element of *déjà vu* with that of *non-sequitur* – whose substance is unsupported by evidence, or is nonsensical or self-contradictory. 'But why should he suddenly say this ?' or 'What does he mean ?' one asks oneself bleakly, having been reading on quite happily until this point. The shameful truth gradually emerges to confront the teacher inescapably. This particular passage is evidently based on part of a lecture he has given on the topic; he had thought it clearly expressed and even interest-provoking. Yet at least one student has completely misunderstood the whole purport of the argument. He has not grasped the point; he is unaware of this failure; he does not query the absurdity of what he is writing; he evidently believes that his teachers will contentedly consume a re-heated hot-pot of half-baked ingredients.

This is a chastening but salutary educational experience for the lecturer, though his efforts have evidently not been very beneficial to the student. It is the kind of external assessment which there is no gainsaying – direct negative validation of his teaching technique, demonstrating that it has been tried and found wanting. This is surely one of the best methods of estimating how successful a given course of teaching has been. In these terms 'success" would be adjudged in a lively, well-argued piece of writing; one which shows evidence of the student's having listened and read, discussed and reflected; showing evidence too of his having *understood* – sufficiently for him to identify with those aspects which he finds acceptable and also to criticise and to branch out beyond those aspects.

It may be an unrealistic counsel of perfection to expect all students to react to their teaching in this way. They vary or course, at least as much as their teachers vary among themselves. But the teachers owe a responsibility to each of their pupils as well as to themselves and their subject matter. And it is suggested that if more than one or two students get hold of completely the wrong end of the stick on any particular topic, in any course, the teacher should become aware of this and should aim to improve his methods. He should shoulder the responsibility and accept the blame, rather than unload it on to the student or on to the abstruseness or novelty of the subject being taught. Although comparisons are unfeasible, as well as odious, it is very likely that some subjects are intrinsically harder than others; some are more difficult to communicate; and some are currently so lacking in factual body – and are changing fashion at such bewildering speed – that it might be argued that no attempt should be made to teach them at present. However, in view of their inevitable popularity, any move to suppress them would probably cause a riot, if not a revolution. In any case, the teaching of such studies is closely linked with research and on these grounds too it just might be a pity to cut down on it. This relationship – between teaching and research, generally – has already been discussed (Chapter IX).

Chapter XIV

Student assessment

'One must learn by doing the thing: for though you
think you know it, you have no certainty until you try.'

SOPHOCLES

The ambiguity of the title of this chapter provides an apt comment
on the climate of university opinion in the second half of the 20th century. During the first six or seven hundred years of university education,
the phrase would have been quite clear. But it now poses the question:
assessment *by* students or assessment *of* students? Since the former has
already been considered (in Chapter XIII) it is with the latter that we are
here concerned. How should students be assessed as to their academic
ability, diligence and attainment? Since many students, and some
university teachers, would drop the 'how' in the preceding question, the
problems as to *whether* and *why* students should be assessed at all is later
discussed.

Means of assessment include the traditional three-hour examination
paper. Here the student knows roughly what topics will be covered in
each paper but he is allowed to take into the examination hall only pen and
pencil (and, where relevant, logarithm tables, lists of basic formulae and
dictionaries). Less traditional forms of examination may involve grant-
ing permission to take a couple of reference books into the examination
hall, or allowing the candidate to visit libraries and to spend much of the
day collecting information for known questions and answering them in a
relatively unhurried manner.

Other means include a single question essay paper; multiple choice
questions; short answer papers; making material available during
examinations; the research project, with its mini dissertation plus –
usually – its *viva voce*; and continuous assessment. There are a few other

methods, such as orals and performance in a language laboratory, for modern linguists; receiving prior information about questions, in some arts subjects; and a long practical examination with open access to notes and books, for pure and applied scientists.* But these latter techniques are used in certain specialized subjects only and will not be referred to again. Let us consider each of the other methods in turn.

The 'single question essay paper' is something of a misnomer since the candidate almost always has a choice of essay topics. The paper is so named because the student is asked to utilize his three hours in writing one essay. The choice is generally from four or more titles. These usually cover a variety of rather general topics, some of which may be loosely linked to the student's main subject; other titles may be quite unrelated to his field of study. If the candidate chooses one of the latter, he is of course free to weave some tenuous connection between the title and his own studies or he is equally at liberty to free-associate to his selected title, producing an essay complete in itself, entirely un-related to his studies.

The aim of this essay paper is to ascertain the fluency, originality and style of the student. Does he have ideas of his own? If so, do they extend beyond his speciality? Has he the courage of his convictions? Has he the courage, and the imagination, to day-dream publicly? Or is he merely brash in so doing? Can he combine his thoughts and his feelings into a harmonious whole? If he elects to write from an intellectual viewpoint only, does he do so in a train-like way, along narrow grooves? – or, more like a bus, along an ungrooved but predictable route? Or is he the rare thinker who, like a sky-diver, moves easily in three dimensions?

These are the sorts of questions asked by the setters of the paper who are, of course, also the readers of the essays. The essay is the one paper in which a sense of relevance is not the over-riding consideration. It provides an opportunity for the candidate to demonstrate his crea-tivity, to show his examiners the type and the degree of constructive imagination he possesses, to indicate his sense of style. In the case of the scientist, it may be the *only* opportunity of this kind, since his other examination papers are likely to be concerned with matters primarily of knowledge.

It is therefore crucial that the titles offered should cover a very wide

---

*I am greatly indebted to Sheffield University for making available to me the Report of their Working Party on Assessment of Students (1972). Much of the information in this chapter derives from their Report.

range of topic and flavour and it is desirable that the examiners, too, should vary in outlook: for the judging of the essay will clearly be to some extent a matter of the examiner's taste. The most 'way-out' essays are liable to be marked very low by one assessor and very highly by another, whilst the candidate who 'plays safe' may well be adjudged as good average by both. The safeguard of having an external examiner is vital for the essay, as indeed it is for all forms of assessment.

Thus, the single question essay paper is essentially subjective to mark. Bearing in mind that subjectivity is liable to reduce both the validity and the consistency of a measure, has it then any redeeming features? I believe that it has; and the Sheffield University survey revealed that a substantial number of students think well of the method. Their reasons for liking it include the following: it allows sufficient time for good work, it yields an indication of general knowledge, it covers a broad range of subjects and is a strong incentive to wider reading.

These are quite good reasons for continuing with an essay paper. But I, personally, would retain it (in all subjects and at all levels) partly on the grounds that the students themselves perceive these as advantages, and partly because I believe that any method should be included which enables originality and imagination to manifest themselves. A discrepancy between the candidate's essay and other papers may be very revealing, especially when it is the essay which is 'anomalously' impressive. This may yield interesting implications concerning special gifts of the student, hitherto unrecognized, his industriousness (or lack of it), or conceivably a hint that he might do better reading another subject.

Multiple-choice questions are at the other end of the spectrum from the single question essay paper. They consist of a great many highly specific questions, each purporting to have a simple correct answer. Every question is followed by a number of proffered solutions – ideally five or six but occasionally as few as three or four (sometimes even a two-fold choice of true/false is offered) – one and only one of which is the right answer. In my view it is ludicrous, in a questionnaire of any kind, to limit the choice to two, since this yields a 50 per cent probability of getting the correct answer purely by chance. Moreover, there are few problems of interest at university level which can be dealt with on a simple true/false basis. A three- or four-fold choice still seems to me too few, since the chance probability remains uncomfortably high and it is therefore necessary to include a very large number of items.

Thus the only multiple-choice papers to be taken seriously, in my view, are those which offer five or six solutions for each question

These so-called 'objective' examinations are sometimes said to be suitable for the more objective subjects, such as mathematics, engineering, and the natural sciences (including medicine). Even enthusiastic proponents of this method are unlikely, in this country, to advocate its use in arts subjects – though it is so used, to some extent, in the USA, which has enormous numbers of students reading arts – and in Britain the technique is not unknown with certain 'black swans' such as social studies and architecture.

When speaking of mathematics and engineering as objective, the epithet requires no quotation marks, since these disciplines have an acknowledged basis of factual knowledge, at least at undergraduate level. There is agreement among the experts in such fields as to what constitutes the subject matter and what are the facts concerning it. This is what I mean by describing such disciplines as objective.

The phrase 'objective examination', however – a phrase often used to denote papers comprising multiple-choice questions – does require quotation marks, since such examinations are objective in a limited sense only. They are so in the consistency with which the answers are scored: no judgment is needed (as in marking essay-type questions) since the correct solutions have merely to be underlined or ringed, and are scored equally competently by an examiner or a clerk or a machine. But it is risky to assume objectivity in all the *questions*. The reduction of knowledge into the stark form, 'what is the answer to n a, b, c, d or c?' results, at best, in over-simplifying and trivializing a topic; at worst, in bewildering the student – often the more able and imaginative student. I was present when a multiple-choice physics paper was passed round a group of scientists and one of the most distinguished physicists there publicly proclaimed that he did not know the intended solution to many of the questions and that, in his opinion, there was no simple answer to many of the questions.

This cannot be dismissed by saying 'that was a poorly designed objective paper: with a little care, they can be made wholly cogent'. The trivializing is, I think, inherent in such papers. But if they are to be rendered fool-proof and genius-proof, they will require an inordinate amount of time and trouble in their preparation – and one of their alleged assets is that they *save* a great deal of time. They clearly do save time in the marking but they demand a lot more time in preparation than is needed in devising traditional type examination questions, laborious though that is.

What do the students think of this type of examination paper?

According to the Sheffield survey, the students who had the greatest experience in taking multiple-choice examinations – and who reacted to these most favourably – were the medical students, clinical and pre-clinical. A small proportion of students in other faculties approved. The most frequent praises were for the elimination of tedious essay writing, the broader range of subjects coverable and – for some strange reason – that the method is useful 'in assessing normal capacity'.

My own feeling is that the multiple-choice method, if employed at all, should be used very sparingly and always in conjunction with essay-type papers – in which case 'the elimination' of tedious essay-writing would be an over-statement, though the extent of such writing might be reduced. The multiple-choice system is either very time-consuming to prepare or largely invalid in practice, and it is liable to penalise precisely the most desirable students – those who are meticulous and critical in their thinking, or inventive and unconventional, or both.

The phrase 'material available during examinations' covers at least two techniques. One consists of allowing the student virtually unlimited access to a library plus his own notes and books; with meal breaks and perhaps the operation of an 'honour system', this procedure tends to cover considerably longer than the standard three hours. The other consists of allowing the students to take books and references of his choice with him into the examination hall for the three-hour period.

The aim of these methods is to reduce strain (due to the customary rigid time-limit and the arbitrariness of the examination questions, as perceived by the candidate) and also to reduce artificiality (due to the intellectual vacuum in which traditional examinations are conducted and thought by some to have no parallel 'in real-life').

In practice, the system of having material available during examinations imposes a greater strain on some students since they feel that, in the circumstances, it is incumbent upon them to get everything right and to omit nothing. Moreover, those who are allowed more than three hours may well find that the longer period is in itself very taxing. There are, in addition, certain practical difficulties in the library procedure, such as demands for the same books being made by a number of candidates simultaneously.

Artificiality of some kind seems unavoidable: any attempt to equate the examination situation with a long-term, 'real-life' situation is, itself, a highly artificial endeavour. In the library method, for instance, the candidates are naturally requested not to communicate with one another. In the 'take your references into the hall with you' system, some students are bound to find that they have made a poor choice – but, unlike most real-life situations, they will not be able to go and fetch the more helpful references.

'Material in examinations' has not proved a very popular system with those students who have tried it. The one virtue claimed by those who liked it is that it involves less rote-learning than does the traditional examination paper. But this claim is based on a misconception, for most university examiners are not looking for parrot-learned material in their examination scripts and tend not to mark it highly when they find it. They are looking for understanding of what has been learned (and understanding involves paraphrasing rather than repetition), for a critique of what has been understood and for original ideas on the subject, provided that these are compatible with the facts.

Little will be said here of the research project as a means of assessment since a previous chapter is wholly devoted to it. In addition to the advantages enumerated in Chapter X, it may be worth stating that many students expressed a liking for it – indeed it proved second in popularity only to continuous assessment. Reasons given for its commendation include, once again, sufficient time for good work, and also better understanding of subject, greater personal achievement, the opportunity of demonstrating originality and initiative, and the reduction of nervous strain.

We come now to the assessment method which, it is claimed, appeals most to students and which is probably the most controversial. I say 'it is claimed' because I have gained the impression through reading and talking with students that, here as elsewhere in education, what is new or different is *ipso facto* deemed better (or perhaps it would be more accurate to say that what is old or traditional is *ipso facto* to be decried). The late Professor Michotte once said, characteristically, that if matches had been invented later than cigarette lighters, the inventor of matches would have been hailed as a genius!

The method of continuous assessment takes into account all the work that the student has produced during his undergraduate days. Thus his weekly essays and discussions with his supervisor – and the end-of-term reports, based on these supervisions and sent to his college tutor – his practicals and resultant notes (whether these be, for instance, practical criticism of English literature or the practicals of chemistry), his contributions in seminars, the conduct of his research project, his discussions with members of staff: any or all of these may form part of the student's continuous assessment. It is realized that few, if any, will have the opportunity of experiencing all the procedures listed above, but those which apply in any particular case are taken into consideration, where the method of continuous assessment is used.

This idea is well-liked by most students. It reduces the near-hysteria which often heralds the approach of 'finals' and it belies the suggestion that 'all the work done in the last three years – and one's whole future career – depends on a few arbitrary three-hour papers'. It provides for the candidate who has a 'genuine' attack of 'flu or indigestion but does not wish to take an *aegrotat* – and, of course, it also provides for those whose ailments at examination time are psychosomatic. It is felt by the student to put less strain on his memory and his nerves, to assess his working capacity under normal conditions and to cause his effort to be spread over a longer, more representative period. He is unimpressed by the argument that it is up to him, whatever the system of assessment, to spread his effort over the whole period he spends at the university.

It can, however, be argued that continuous assessment puts a greater strain on the student because it allows no let-up throughout the term; that some students need to lie dormant for weeks at a time in order to emerge refreshed and free from confusion (on continuous assessment such behaviour might appear, pejoratively, as 'erratic'); that the system imposes stress on the relationship between student on the one hand, and tutor or supervisor on the other; indeed that it puts unhealthy pressure on the university staff to appraise at the same time as they teach and encourage them to crystallize their appraisal at too early a stage – bearing in mind the difficulty experienced in revising one's opinion of somebody, once having made up one's mind.

Finally, a word should perhaps be said on behalf of the able student who, for whatever reason, works little during most of his university days but who possesses the capacity and stamina to concentrate fiercely just before his final examination and has also the intelligence and organizing ability to show his excellence in a series of three-hour papers. Such students – if they are assessed continuously throughout their university career, and only so assessed – might fare poorly.

Having discussed most of the other means of assessing students, a word should be said about the traditional three-hour paper. We have seen that it is currently denigrated on grounds of unfairness (to the slow, the nervous and the ill), of artificiality, of arbitrariness (in terms of the questions set), and of setting too high a premium on speed of writing. In my opinion many of these criticisms are over-stressed. To consider them jointly: the slow, the nervous and the ill are very often penalized in 'real life'. Therefore to penalize them in an examination may be thought realistic rather than artificial. Moreover, to allow such disabilities to work to the advantage of the sufferer is – to use a psychological term – *to reinforce* the disabilities. There are many situations outside the ivory tower where reasonable speed and *mens sana in corpore sano* are desirable. As to the arbitrariness of the questions set, this criticism ignores the fact that university examinations almost always provide a generous choice of questions. Three or four questions to be selected by the candidate from eight or ten is customary, the examiners usually taking care to cover the syllabus but not go beyond it. In these circumstances it cannot often be true that the candidate who comes out saying 'not a decent question in the whole paper' is entirely justified. Lastly, 'slowness in writing' is often a euphemism for slowness in thinking. The latter may well be a hindrance in real-life situations.

Examination taking (like university teaching) is a skill and, this being so, the student needs to keep in practice. I would suggest, therefore, that examinations should be held annually, whatever discipline or combinations of disciplines the student is reading. This will keep him in training and it will diminish the alarm aroused at the onset of an examination held after a two- or three-year period in which no examination of any importance is taken.

I believe that the traditional examination should be retained as a means of student assessment but that other means should also be used, notably continuous assessment and the research project for those students to whom it appeals. This system is not only fair: it would also be seen to be fair – if the student is suitably informed soon after he arrives at the university. The inference generally should be that a student is as good as he shows himself to be *at his best* – whether his best happens to be in a *viva voce*, a three-hour paper or on continuous assessment. Such discrepancies as appear are likely to be instructive with respect to the student's temperament and vocation.

There is no danger that on such a system 'all students will turn out to be brilliant' – a fear that is sometimes expressed by those who feel that the truth is extracted from people only if the means be thoroughly unpleasant and the worst possible interpretation put upon the findings. Differentiation will still be achieved but, I submit, more validly than when strictly traditional means alone are used for the purpose. The case for student-assessment, that is, for effecting differentiation among students, is made in the next Chapter.

Chapter XV

Why educate? And why assess?

'The real object of education is to leave a man in the
condition of continually asking questions.'
                                    Bishop CREIGHTON

The question 'why educate' seems to be closely related to the question
raised in Chapter XIII, 'what is successful teaching?' But though
intimately related, they are not the same thing. A successful teacher,
it was suggested, stimulates and challenges his pupils; he invites
participation in his lectures and accepts criticism of them; his lectures
are reasonably well-attended. He is intelligible – or, if his students fail
to understand him they are aware of this and, as a good teacher, he
welcomes their awareness and creates an opportunity to elucidate
matters. In a word, he effects two-way communication.

This reply, however, does not answer the wider question, 'why
educate?' The latter question raises the whole issue as to what is the
value of education, whom should we educate, up to what level – what,
indeed, is meant by the term 'education'. In the last chapter we discussed some of the methods by which university students are assessed.
In this chapter it is hoped that a link between education and assessment
may be forged and that an argument may be made for assessment as
such.

Education means all things to all men. To the educated it signifies a
broader gateway to the enjoyment of many of the good things in life:
enhanced enjoyment of literature – light and heavy, literary and scientific, philosophical and poetic; of the arts – painting, sculpture, music,
drama, architecture; of the elegance and simplicity born of complex
scientific theories; of social intercourse and friendship with a wider
variety of people; even of the more sensuous aspects of life, such as sex

and food and drink. To the under-educated it often signifies, rightly or wrongly, a means to a better – or a less constrained – job and a higher material standard of living.

To the over-educated, i.e. those whose years of study or strings of qualifications exceed their native ability and their intellectual curiosity, it provides opportunities for one-upmanship and the proud parade of an 'academic mind'. These may be met in all walks of life including, alas, universities. They are recognizable by their reluctance to use a monosyllabic word if a polysyllabic one be available, their belief that their didactic prowess is invariably more edifying than that of their companions and their confusion of esoteric learning with wisdom. They might be described as educational failures and, as such, they are very instructive in the search for educational aims. Education has not 'taken' with them, though they often demonstrate excellent recall of what they have been taught, they may be knowledgeable on a number of topics and are highly articulate.

What then do they lack? They have not learned to appreciate other people's points of view and they can therefore never fully savour the delights of personal discussion and shared interests; their near-total recall precludes them from the pleasurable exercise of selection – they tend to be all-or-none on most subjects; they have not acquired a sense of relevance; they have not learned the humility and sensitivity which should accompany increased learning; they have little sense of proportion and of humour; they take themselves too seriously; they tend to lack tolerance and to be intellectual snobs.

Thus, they are, in their deficiencies, very instructive as to what the goals of higher education are, or should be. One such goal is to widen the horizons of the student, that is, to increase his own capacity – for the appreciation of rightness in whatever sphere. 'Rightness' here covers, with its customary generosity, factual correctness, scientific elegance, literary and artistic beauty and ethical soundness. Another aim is the increase also of this capacity in others. I speak of widening the horizons 'of the student', for a further function of education is to instil the realization that education enables one to remain a student, able and willing to learn, all one's life.

Evidently, education should teach also the joys and the dangers of generalizing. Just as acquiring a second language facilitates the acquisition of a third, so the learning of one discipline facilitates the learning of others. This involves a kind of generalizing. Yet the more successfully educated are apt to become increasingly aware of the risks of making sweeping generalizations on more specific subjects. This is a failing to which the over-educated, and also the under-educated, are prone: the xenophobe, the anti-semite, the colour-prejudiced, tend to emanate from their ranks rather than from those of the well-educated.

The latter point is associated with learning to avoid hyperbolic and authoritarian assertions. It is much easier to produce extreme statements than many-faceted or middle-of-the-road observations. It is also easier to attract attention and be provocative by talking in superlatives and drawing invidious distinctions than it is by restricting oneself to balanced views. One of the aims of education is surely to inculcate a love of rationality and fair-mindedness without any loss in spontaneity and vividness. Aristotle's golden mean has not lost its lustre over the centuries.

Associated with this is the educational function of learning to reconcile the emotional with the rational, when these conflict in one's work, indeed in life generally. To attempt to deny the existence of value judgments and emotions – as do some academics in some disciplines – surely indicates a failure of understanding on their part. If these vigorous and ever-present factors are to play their role they must be admitted and incorporated into what is being studied and taught. Otherwise they are liable to pervade the work and subtly to distort it.

Close to this, too, is the development of a sense of responsibility – to others and also to oneself. The successfully educated are not heavy solemn beings who smile rarely and laugh never. But they understand the priorities and one of these is keeping faith with themselves, their friends – and their adversaries.

Lastly, the well-educated will have assimilated a good deal of information in their chosen field and probably in allied fields. The word 'assimilated' is used here in order to convey the idea of the student himself developing with his intake of knowledge. If he is successfully educated, the metaphor is not that of a rigid, metallic receptacle into which more and more facts are poured; it is rather of some flexible, porous body which, like the amoeba, will change shape and size as it absorbs nutriment.

This informational aspect of education is mentioned last because it is considered necessary though not sufficient. If the student has failed to attain much knowledge but has stretched his intellectual curiosity and learned the means of satisfying it, has acquired interest in ideas and their application, tolerance of varied views and varied people – in a word, if he has learned to think – there is hope for him.

The essence of successful education is that the individual remains intellectually forward-looking, whatever his age.

So far we have considered the question 'why educate?' from the viewpoint of the recipient of education. If the above suggestions be acceptable, it is likely that the well-educated individual will, by virtue of his habits of mind, influence others beneficially rather than deleteriously – though exceptions do occur. But the question as to what society as a whole derives from its highly educated minority also merits discussion. Society offers ever-increasing financial support to higher education. What, if anything, does it gain from its outlay?

In theory, it should benefit, in the long run, both economically and culturally. Let us briefly consider each of these in turn. The economic benefits accrue mainly from educational investment in technology and applied science – although, as suggested in Chapter IX, the line between pure and applied is often hard to draw. Research and teaching in these fields has produced such vast developments as space research, resulting in new techniques of communications (for instance, intercontinental satellite telephone links) and better weather prediction (still leaving room for improvement, but it is better than it was). Work in nuclear physics promises some constructive results in the fields of energy resources and of medicine. In the sphere of applied biology, one of the greatest advances is in contraceptive methods which are simple to use, relatively cheap, and acceptable to most members of most societies. The social and economic gains to the community in these areas hardly need elaborating. The improved utilization of materials and men increases productivity, world trade and leisure opportunities.

Economic advantages are derived also from non-scientific studies. It is the graduates in English and modern languages who teach the skills necessary for communicating within the whole social fabric – nationally and internationally. Moreover, industrial management culls many of its members from arts faculties.

The specifically cultural benefits which society gains from its support of higher education are, of course, less tangible and they stem notably more from the humanities and the fine arts than from science. A society which neglects these spheres may well decline, and considerable repute is gained by those nations which produce, and are proud to produce, internationally renowned artists and musicians, writers and journalists, philosophers and statesmen. Some of these – though by no means all – have had the benefit of a university education.

Now that some answer has been offered to the question 'why educate?'

we can consider the question 'why assess?' It is fashionable in many quarters to disparage the whole notion of assessment with its implications of differentiation among individuals – and, hence, discrimination in its pejorative sense. It is largely on these grounds that university (and other) examinations are censured and that other methods are being sought to replace them.

The argument goes: 'there aren't really four clearcut types of student – first classes, second classes, third classes and failures. They are all students and they must have been pretty good to get into university.' At this point the argument may branch one of two ways. Either, the line is taken that those who are *not* pretty good should not have been admitted to university in the first place – blame then falling on the selectors; or the line is taken that everybody who wishes to do so has the right to a university education and, it follows, a right to a (one-class) degree.

The argument is rarely spelt out as crudely as this. What is implicit, however, and not spelt out at all, is the dogma that assessment is intrinsically offensive because it grades some people poorly: whenever assessment takes place, some individuals will be rated as 'below average' and this is not to be borne. Presumably the discrediting of examinations is due largely to the fact that they traditionally do rank candidates in several grades; and presumably the unconscious hope in exploring vaguer and newer means is, partly, that these will result in vaguer and less definite divisions. This is certainly true, for instance, of continuous assessment which often takes the form, 'his work has improved over the last few weeks' or 'she does better in personal discussion than in written work' or 'I anticipate marked progress next term'.

Of course it is true that there are not four (or five or six) clearcut types of student, nor would any examiner wish to claim that there were. The existence of some 'border-line' candidates is acknowledged and examiners take a great deal of trouble, individually and jointly, over them: 'Must we fail him or can we just give him a third? . . . He has gained a high second on all his papers – could we perhaps give him a first?' . . . and so on. Students naturally do not fall into well-separated categories, but neither do they all possess the same ability, knowledge, and capacity to work to good effect. They range from the outstandingly able to the relatively dull, with the majority falling well within these two extremes. (Statistically, almost all students fall within the top 15–20 per cent of the nation's ability.) Any system of assessment which fails to bring out this range is not fulfilling its function. The very existence of 'good students' entails the existence of weaker students. If every student is equal, academically, to every other, then there are no good students.

If, then, the argument against assessment is founded on the basic equality of university students, or on the suggestion that whilst some are better, none are worse; or on the belief then there is something inherently degrading and unfair about assessment as such, I find these arguments unconvincing. They seem to be rationalizations made by rather unthinking critics who dislike the idea that they – or their teachers or their students – might be assessed as less able than their rivals. Some critics go so far as to condemn all competition as wrong and to attribute many of the ills of our society to its highly competitive nature. This is indeed quite consistent with the censuring of assessment.

The onus of proof, then, is on the defender of student assessment. Does it serve any useful functions? And, if so, what are they? One evident function is to provide some kind of guide to the student's future employer. Some graduates know what they wish to do on leaving university, others have little idea. Some, such as engineers or medics, may wish to make use of the specialized knowledge they have gained as a student; others may wish to join the Civil Service or to enter industry, specifically not using the skills they have learned – or, at least, not in any direct way; others elect to become school teachers; yet others wish to take some further training, either in a field related to their degree subject or in some quite dissimilar field.

There are many other possibilities. But in those listed above and in many others, the graduate will be required to show what he has gained from his university education. His degree class is likely to be thought relevant for two reasons: first, to show what standard of excellence he has attained in the subject(s) of his choice and, secondly, to compare him with the other graduate-applicants. Selection implies rejection; in most fields of graduate-entry there are more candidates than vacancies and the potential employer will, if he is wise, take into account as many pointers as possible. These pointers will probably include an interview in which the student will have a chance to speak for himself and to show his appearance, manner and personal suitability; he will also learn something of the appropriateness of the potential employer; references will probably be followed up, anything from one to three university referees being approached; and his degree class will almost certainly be contained in his dossier.

Many employers are aware of the problems of comparing the value of degree classes from different universities. They are aware too that many students and staff members do not regard the degree class as the be-all and end-all of university life. Indeed, employers not infrequently assert that they prefer the graduate with outside interests, or with social flair, or the athlete, to the successful 'swot'. The emphasis varies with the job and with the employer but, since he is electing to employ a graduate, he will in any case wish to know what class was obtained in the university examination if only to weigh this against other data.

A situation in which student-assessment has a more clearly pertinent function is that in which the graduate wishes to go on to research and university teaching. It was suggested at the beginning of this book that teaching ability is not necessarily a concomitant of high quality scholarship. Such scholarship is, however, an essential ingredient in the recipe for a good university teacher and also for a fruitful research worker. In general, research grants cannot be obtained for graduates who fail to gain a first or an upper second. It is true that an occasional lower second does manage to enter research and to do well but he will have had quite exceptional strings pulled on his behalf – because he is that rare bird, the student who has dramatically failed to do himself justice in his final examination and who is recognized by his university teachers to have so failed. These exceptional cases should not be taken to imply that degree class bears no relation to research ability: it clearly does. The inference is rather that the system works well in that it is not wholly inflexible and that it allows the potential researcher who is keen, determined and also did have bad luck in his examination, to try his hand at it. It also underlines the fact that 'continuous assessment' is far from new and has occasionally played an overriding role.

This brings us to a third function of student-assessment – a more 'student-centred' function than those which have been considered. It is an incentive – if not a major one, nowadays – to the individual during his years at university to know that the effort he has put into his work is going to be soberly and impartially assessed, at the end of his course; and that he will leave university with a qualification deemed by the community to have some significance. All being well, he will have a university degree and he will be officially 'classed' with what is still generally thought to have some degree of objectivity. This is a carrot, rather than a stick, sensed with increasing clarity as he wends his way through his three or four years of study and good-fellowship, of social, sexual, political and intellectual development.

This is the forward-looking aspect: knowing that official student-assessment awaits him at the end of his course. Many would feel let-down if they were suddenly informed that no such assessment would be made. There is also the retrospective viewpoint, the student feedback aspect of assessment. Most of us like receiving information as to how we are viewed by others; even unflattering assessment is better than being ignored or indistinguishable from everybody else.

Apart from feeling interested and sometimes gratified when they learn their results, some students even wait until they learn their degree-class before making up their mind what career to aim for. I am not thinking here of the 'drop-outs' and the 'eternal students', the small minority who will seize every opportunity of postponing a decision, and maintaining the *status quo*, as long as is financially possible. I have in mind the genuinely open-minded ('I'd like to do x if I get a good enough degree but, if not, I'll do y'), and the modest ('I hope to do z if I've done well enough – I'll have to see') and the realistic ('I'm hoping to get a place at w but that will depend mainly on my examination results and my referees').

There is also the strictly psychological angle of the student's involvement with his finals. They are rightly seen as a great challenge, producing ambivalence and a powerful flow of adrenalin; the fact that his friends and acquaintances are similarly threatened adds to the mixed spiciness of the situation; tension mounts, communally and individually, until the onset of examinations – and at the end of them is a wonderful sense of release. The whole experience is memorable and is treasured by some students to the end of their days.

Those who consider this an exaggerated and romanticized account of the university examination ritual – who have forgotten the trauma, the heady excitement and the eventual relief – are those whom custom has staled: those who, having cleared this initial hurdle, go on to take higher examinations and then, themselves, become university examiners. They grow used to seeing generation after generation of young people live through this experience, and after a few years they may lose their capacity to empathize, to recall and to imagine. It is an experience, however, which is new and real for each undergraduate; and – asked five or ten years later whether they would retrospectively opt out of it – I suspect that most would give a negative reply.

The next, and last, function of student-assessment again concerns feedback but this time the feedback is for university teachers, supervisors and tutors, for the universities and the colleges. Earlier in this chapter the aims of education were discussed. The aims as stated may well be controversial: some may find them too wide, others too limited; some may consider that they place too little emphasis on scholarship, whilst others may hold that the specifically scholarly aims are overstated. All who have thought about higher education pay lip-service to the notion that there is more to university life than mere academic learning; many who say this actually believe it; and quite a few behave as though they believe it.

Despite this, only a small minority of academics would actively strive for the abolition of university examinations and an even smaller minority would agree to do away with student-assessment generally. Moreover these small minorities belong, I believe, to unrepresentative university departments and egregious political persuasions. Considering the immense amount of time and trouble that examinations demand of setters and markers, it is worth asking why the consensus of opinion is that they should be retained. Cynical answers along the lines of hire-worthy labourers and time otherwise hanging heavy, are non-starters. Examining is not well-paid, and most academics greatly prefer the activities of research and teaching to that of examining.

They need, however, to learn how well they are fulfilling their function as educators. They can learn, as examiners – not what they and other university teachers have actually said in their lectures, but what they have been understood to say. Those who are not examining can learn whether the students whom they have supervised or directed are ranked in roughly the same order in examinations as they would be ranked on the basis of essays, discussions and research projects. It is interesting, too, to see how one's own pupils compare with those supervised by other members of staff; to see which examination questions have been the most popular – and the best answered – an intercorrelation which is not always high; to hear from the students what they felt about the examination and its results.

This kind of feedback is necessary if higher education is to justify itself to outside bodies: to learn from its failures and successes. Of additional, minor interest is the comparison of student sub-groups, according to discipline, sex and college (where relevant). It is interesting to observe, for instance, that women students are liable to obtain relatively more seconds than men, the male students gaining generally more firsts and more thirds; and that this tends to hold in most faculties and most universities.

Since much of this chapter has been concerned with one particular method of assessment, the examination, a brief discussion of its merits – as opposed to those of other methods – would not be misplaced. University examinations offer the candidate considerable freedom of choice, adequate forewarning being given in the occasional situation of one or two questions being compulsory. This freedom is attained by offering a number of papers covering different aspects of the discipline, all of these comprising more questions than the candidate is asked to tackle. A general essay paper is nearly always included. Thus the student has the opportunity of showing what he has learned, remembered and understood; of stating and defending his own ideas on a variety of subjects; and of demonstrating his powers of self-expression.

Of great value in university examinations is the practice of having at least one external examiner. He brings to the task his own standards and, being unacquainted with the candidates, he has no prejudices for or against any individuals.

The objections to examinations are well-known. They are sometimes said to lack consistency – in the test-retest sense – and it is rightly asked how any criterion which lacks consistency can be valid. The other arguments against examinations usually concentrate on the effects of nervous tension in the students – that this is itself to be deprecated, that it detracts from the value of the exercise and that it penalizes candidates unevenly, hence unjustly.

There is undoubtedly some substance in these criticisms. The unstated assumptions, however, are rarely stated or even recognized. Are examinations being (a) compared with other methods of assessment, as described in Chapter XIV? Or (b) are they being criticised *in vacuo* that is, compared with some hypothetical, ideal technique – which does not exist? In answer to question (a), I should say that it is desirable to employ other methods – to supplement the examination system, not to replace it. A frequent answer to (b) is that examinations and other methods of assessment should go, since all such methods are unsatisfactory and assessment as such is deemed to be unnecessary.

That problem is what this chapter is about: indeed it is what the whole book is about. University teachers need to learn their job, and being assessed is itself an essential constituent of learning. Similarly students, at university and elsewhere, need to learn along the lines indicated earlier in this chapter (most of them, indeed *want* to learn) and for them, too, being assessed is part of the process. It is suggested that it is an integral part. There is nothing revolutionary about this suggestion: it has long been assumed that feedback enormously hastens and strengthens any learning process. This was confirmed by experimental psychologists some decades back, the tasks being somewhat more artificial and the terminology more old-fashioned. What is now known as 'feedback' was then called 'knowledge of results'. The change in terms reflects the change in emphasis from conscious awareness to mechanistic behaviour – a regrettable change, in my view – but the message is the same. We learn better if we know how well (or poorly) we are doing, and if we know wherein lie our deficiencies.

Students are well aware of this, hence their willingness in general to take part in assessment procedures of their teachers. In so doing, they help the teachers and, if not themselves, at least future generations of students. Most students would feel cheated if they too were not assessed; and most of them realize that the results of such assessment must be made public, if its other functions are to be fulfilled.

Chapter XVI

Why yet another book on university teaching?

'Some books are to be tasted, others to be swallowed, and some few to be chewed and digested.'

Francis BACON

The bibliography on pages 133 and 134 is a list selected from a proliferation of books and reports on the subject of university teaching – some of which I have not seen and few of which I have read from cover to cover. The question thus arises, why perpetrate yet another publication on this topic? The answer is twofold. First I am somewhat critical of those pamphlets and books which I have read, especially those which have appeared within the last few years. Secondly, I hope that I have something new to contribute – or at least that the particular combination of ideas which I put forward denotes an approach which differs from the *laissez faire, laissez aller*, anti-assessment type of 'progressive education', on the one hand, and the traditional type of authoritarian, teaching-plus-examining, on the other.

I must admit, too, the hope that my style of writing is less turgid than that of my predecessors in the field. Much of the recent literature on 'tertiary education' as it is characteristically called, deals with it in a cut and dried, statistical manner, abounding in flow-charts, percentages, tables and frequency distributions; and, not only for that reason, it often makes heavy reading.

Whilst realizing (even explicitly asserting, see Chapter IV) that material to be read needs a presentation different from material to be heard, I nonetheless hold that reading matter should be lucid and smooth-flowing, as long as this entails no over-simplification and no loss of information or essential details. This seems to me especially important when the writer is offering instruction on *how to teach*. Much of the literature I have studied suffers from verbosity, a profusion of scientific jargon and emphasis on 'experimentation' the relevance of which is sometimes less than obvious.

An experiment is reported, for instance, in which a 45 minute lecture is divided into three periods of, respectively, 15 minutes, 30 minutes and 45 minutes; and comparison is made between the amount of information retained by the listeners who heard only the first quarter-hour, that retained by those who heard the first half-hour and by those who heard the full 45 minute lecture.[17, quoted in 3] The estimate of material remembered in such experiments is usually made soon after the end of the lecture – very likely by means of a multiple-choice test or even a true-false questionnaire. My specific objections to such methods will become clear later.

Such experimentation in general is typical of that of many sociologists, psychologists and other social scientists. They believe, understandably, that they are particularly well-suited to investigate these problems. Moreover, they appear to hold that quantitative treatment of data constitutes scientific study – however artificially collated or arbitrarily interpreted the data may be. Often the participating students are themselves in one of the social science disciplines. They have the virtue of being conveniently to hand for the experiment but the defect of being, probably, unrepresentative of the student population as a whole.

In other reported experiments the collaborators and their teachers are American – although the conventions, and to some extent the aims, of universities in the USA differ markedly at undergraduate level from those in Britain. I have the impression that American teachers in universities and colleges generally set more store by attendance at lectures, absorption of communicated facts and conscientious regurgitation of those – and less on the capacity of students to think for themselves, to appraise critically and to demonstrate constructive originality – than do English teachers.

Reports of the above kind show a breathtaking naiveté. They are based on a number of presuppositions which are not stated or apparently even recognized and which are eminently questionable. Since many of these assumptions are implicit in other recent studies of the lecture method [e.g. 11] it is worth teasing them out and scrutinizing them.

The most important assumption which recurs repeatedly is that the main purpose of the lecture is to *impart information*. Donald Bligh actually goes so far as to state categorically that 'stimulating student interest in a subject should not normally be the major objective of a lecture, because the method is usually ineffective for this purpose'. This assertion is based on some fifteen pages of Tables, summarizing over a hundred English and American surveys. He also invokes animal studies such as Harlow's work 'rewarding monkeys and children for selecting the odd one out of three objects'!

Far from being 'proved' by these surveys, the assumption is highly controversial. As I have suggested earlier, a case can be made for using the lecture method to stimulate and to arouse interest as well as to convey information. Of course these two functions do, ideally, go together. But if they are to be theoretically separated, it seems to me that the reading of books and articles by the students, in their own time, is the better way to acquire knowledge of facts and theories – apart from those which are so newly discovered or propounded that they are not yet to be found in the literature.

A further questionable assumption is that the three selected clusters of listener (15 min., 30 min., and 45 min.) are strictly comparable. The lecture was designed as a 45-minute talk: thus it had, presumably, a '45-minute shape'. If one is giving a 15-minute or a 30-minute talk, one plans the shape appropriately for these differing durations. Thus the conclusion – 'A week later it was found that those hearing only the first 15 minutes recalled twice as much as those who heard the whole 45 minutes' – is suspect in itself, and even more so if it is made the basis of a generalization concerning the optimum length of time for a lecture.

Equally suspect, it seems to me, are those conclusions based on psychological 'tests of personality' as to which types of student fare better on which types of instruction. We are told, for instance, that 'high-drive introverts usually perform better in examinations than low-drive extraverts';[5,7,10] that 'those above the mean on neuroticism (which may reflect anxiety levels) valued lecturers who "speak slowly enough for full notes to be taken" and who "set a standard which students can aim to achieve", more highly than those below the mean';[16] and that the '"quietists" are utilitarians who strongly favour formal methods in schools',[11] These 'quietists' incidentally are described as 'stable, tough-minded Conservatives with a philistine, conformist outlook'. The use of terms as value-laden as 'philistine', and as vague as 'tough-minded', immediately make one surmise that the typologies tell the reader more about the author than about the students he is characterizing.

A great deal of this 'typological' work has been done and it is nearly all based on questionnaires of very doubtful validity. The results of questionnaires, even when well-designed, have to be interpreted with care: they invite leg-pulling or – as the psychometrists put it – 'social desirability response style'. The traits which such tests allegedly assess are usually defined operationally. Thus 'introversion' or 'neuroticism', for instance, are defined in terms of certain arbitrarily determined test-scores (obtained by a small minority) on these naive questionnaires. Such tests are an attempt to 'measure' subtle and intimate facets of personality by a blunt instrument, in wholly inadequate time – sometimes as little as 20–30 minutes. Sooner or later, the operational approach is abandoned and the inference is made that the gainer of a high score on 'introversion' is, *in fact*, a quiet, retiring, rather unsociable individual, more interested in himself than in others, and that the gainer of a high score on 'neuroticism' is, in fact, neurotic.

The abandonment of the operational approach is, of course, readily understandable since nobody would be much interested in personality test scores *per se* and their interrelationships. But the transit from 'operational' to 'real life' is usually effected with masterly unobrusiveness. In this way the experimenter is able to enjoy the best of both worlds – the scientific (since operationalism has a laboratory flavour) and the practical (since concepts such as degree of sociability, and of anxiety, concern us all in our day-to-day lives).

To make the leap from these poorly validated 'experimental types' to suggestions for appropriate teaching seems artlessly optimistic and singularly ill-advised. I give two illustrations of this to show that I am not exaggerating or fabricating. *1.* Evidence is claimed (from the field of mathematics) that 'extraverts learned better when an example was presented before a general rule was adduced, while introverts preferred to be given the rule first and then an example of its application'.[18] *2.* 'After practically no rest, extraverts remember almost twice as much as do introverts. After five minutes, the two groups remember about the same amount. After 24 hours, introverts remember almost twice as much as extraverts. . . . *Most people* are in fact between the two extremes. . . .'[6] – italics by the present writer who wonders why such an immense amount is written about the unrepresentative, small minority comprising alleged extraverts and introverts. Even were the distinction well-proven, it would be hardly realistic to propose one method for teaching the former, a second method for teaching the latter – and, presumably, yet a third method for the big majority who constitute the 'middle' section. The same cavils apply to the many other divisions of people into psychological types: that, first, the principle of different forms of teaching for different sub-groups is not practicable and, secondly, that – whatever the particular typology – it applies only to a small minority at the extreme end of the scale.

A further presupposition made in the work outlined above, deserves comment. This is evident belief that lecturing proficiency can be gauged by ascertaining how much information is retained by the student, shortly after the end of the lecture, by means of the multiple-choice technique or by one-sentence answers. I cordially disagree with this threefold assumption. Such a method might be defensible as an occasional exercise, in junior schools – rather because the children may enjoy the procedure as a sort of game in which they get immediate knowledge of results, than because it provides some measure of the teacher's skill. But to use this method at university level brings into question the whole problem of what higher education is about (which is discussed in Chapters XIII–XV).

First, for most subjects read at British universities, multiple-choice items are inappropriate owing to the inevitable over-simplification and trivialization which they demand. They limit the kind of problem which can be asked and, even when such limitations have been recognized, a consensus of opinion on the correct answer does not always obtain. As stated earlier, I have seen a group of scientists in heated argument as to which of certain responses were 'right' in a multiple-choice physics paper. If this can happen in the physical sciences, how much more questionable is the technique in the biological, philosophical, social or arts fields ? Such papers may positively penalize some students – not only the nonconforming and original, but also those with the misfortune to have a little extra knowledge or to have reflected on the subject.

Secondly, the university lecturer (and, indeed, the school teacher) is aiming to communicate ideas of long-lasting significance to his listeners. He is concerned with what they will recall (and discuss and meditate upon) a term, or a couple of years later. Some teachers influence one for the whole of one's life. To estimate, then, the success of a lecture within hours or days of its delivery is surely irrelevant: it suggests a strange view of the purpose of the lecture and of education generally.

Thirdly, the question of *the amount of information* retained – assessed by whatever means after whatever period – whilst of some educational import, is surely not the whole story. I shall return to this later, in the more positive part of the chapter. For the present I must continue my critique. Those books and reports which I have studied on university teaching, and on the lecture-method in particular, seem to me to contain more than their fair share of statements which are unclear, or trite, or mutually contradictory. In these cases the reading is unlikely to prove valuable to the potential teacher, whether he is in search of interesting theory or of practical advice. Let me give a few examples. (a) Unclear: 'He verified that the forgetting of lecture material was of a lawful character, the curve of forgetting starting at something of the order of 60 per cent on immediate recall and declining to about 20 per cent of remembered material after eight weeks.'(9 quoted in 3)

(b) Trite: 'Whatever our objectives in lecturing, they can only be achieved subject to the psychological limitations of the students.'(3) 'More attention is drawn to a fact if it is repeated . . . "the capital city of the Boyaca province is . . . Tunja . . . Tunja" ', or 'I want to give you three facts . . . three facts'.(12) For the reader who objects that such repetition merits the epithet 'soporific' rather than 'trite', I offer the following: 'If a general point involves "levers", a "fulcrum" and "weights", and the example is a see-saw with two children on it, the lecturer would need to make it explicit that "the children are the weights . . . etc." ' Yes, this is drawn from a book on university lecturing.

(c) Mutually contradictory: The following two sentences are taken from one and the same paragraph in a 60-page pamphlet on lecturing. *1.* 'A vital point which must be insisted upon in any discussion of university teaching methods is that the lecturer *as such* cannot be categorised simply as "instructor-centred", "oracular", "subject-oriented", or in similar terminology.' (italics, as in the original) *2.* 'On the basis of an extremely detailed, first hand study of lecturers in action she [L. G. Wispe] discovered a *meaningful descriptive* dimension to be "directive/non-directive" teaching style.' (Present writer's italics.)

Or again, found on two consecutive pages in the same book: *1.* 'By the use of [the lecture] the scholar can readily inspire an audience with his own enthusiasm; he can capture the imagination of his auditors with the relationship of his special field to human destiny and human purposes; he can communicate the latest results of the painstaking efforts of his fellow-scholars to come to terms with the practical and theoretical problems which bear on man's present and future estate. The lecture method enables him to achieve these ends with the utmost economy of means.' *2.* 'The feedback at present provides evidence that the lecture system is not acceptable in modern times.'

I cannot refrain from one last quotation, although it is not readily categorized as unclear, trite or contradictory. 'The fact that some lecturers are better than others implies that there are lecturing skills that can be learned (unless they are inherited, which seems unlikely!)'! (First exclamation mark in the original; second by the present writer.)

My impression, then, is that much of the writing on university teaching is inconclusive; it is sometimes painfully obvious, yet sometimes lacking in clarity; often it is pedantic and prolix, inappropriate in form, and its data are derived from sources whose pertinence is marginal if not non-existent. These last points seem to me particularly unfortunate when the writer is concerned with teaching how to teach. If a book or a lecture is about teaching, it should surely exemplify those qualities which are desirable in teaching. If these qualities include clarity, vividness, the ability to stimulate, and to arouse curiosity, an ever-vigilant sense of relevance and such brevity as is consistent with comprehensiveness – then these qualities should be manifest in the literature and in the lectures. If the teaching material lacks these characteristics then, I submit, the teacher should – like the physician – heal himself.

I should like to end where I began – with the lecture – for this is largely what university teaching is about and it would, I think, be a pity if this form of teaching fell into disuse. My suggestions are that lectures should continue to be given, but that instead of being almost always of the 'oracular' or monologue type they should take the form largely of public discussion, that is, that the lecturer should elicit participation from his listeners. It follows from this that the lecture should be spoken, as opposed to being read aloud, and that the teacher will sometimes not have time to deliver all that he had planned for the session – since he will have prepared enough material to last the full 50–55 minutes, in case no contributions were forthcoming from his audience. In no circumstances should he hold the floor for longer than 55 minutes.

This form of lecture possesses some of the advantages of the seminar, notably that some of the students – and these are self-selected – take an active part in the proceedings, and all present feel that they are participating in a 'live' performance. The atmosphere is very different from that of the traditional lecture in which some snooze, some take sporadic notes, some (in the guise of note-taking) write an essay that is overdue, some read the newspaper and some chat or play noughts and crosses with their neighbour. I am not suggesting that any of these are nefarious activities: they are all seemly at an appropriate time and place – but not in a lecture theatre during a lecture. But I do wish to suggest that these practices would dramatically decrease in frequency if lecturers changed their style: from the 'oracular' to the participatory, from the set-piece to the spontaneous, from the 'I'm telling you' to the 'let's find out together'.

Such lectures differ from the seminar in many ways. In particular, everybody is expected to speak in a seminar, whereas only a small minority have the chance, or the inclination, in a big group. But the members of this minority often speak for a sizeable sample of the silent members.

Linked with the idea of the lecture-as-discussion is the further idea that the lecturer should not be used exclusively to purvey factual knowledge. Indeed, I am suggesting that he should be so used only when the information has not yet found its way into the literature. The student who seeks knowledge of facts or theories can find it – guided by his teachers – in the textbooks and the journals. What he is less likely to find there is the swift pro and con, the admission of controversy and the outspoken criticism which lends interest to learning and which points the way to the future. If teachers are often backward-looking, students are usually forward-looking, and co-operation between them is likely to lead to a balanced outlook. This seems to me to be one of the ends of education.

In the next chapter I consider the question of ends in relation to means, with special reference to education, and the paradox inherent in the notion of freedom of speech and instruction.

Chapter XVII

Loose ends and loose means

> 'The university must protect itself from those groups within it who, in the pursuit of this freedom for themselves, deny it to others.'
>
> Geoffrey CASTON

In a final chapter, the writer should cast an eye over what has been said and tie any ends which have been left limply hanging. Perhaps the first loose end is the title, *Teaching & Learning in Higher Education*. This has the drawback of lacking brevity and, therefore, punch: but it became clear as the book grew that the original title, *University Teaching*, implied a narrowness of viewpoint that would be misleading. Moreover, the present title conveys, it is hoped, the fact that teaching and learning are two faces of the same coin and the notion that this dual process is two-way – the learning role applying simultaneously to the teacher and the student.

In writing especially the first half of this book I have had very much in mind teaching in Colleges of Education, Colleges of Further Education, Technical Colleges and Polytechnics – and also public lectures and the giving of papers at Congresses and Conferences. It may seem over-ambitious to offer advice simultaneously to all of these yet I feel, unrepentantly, that the call to be lively and stimulating, audible and intelligible, and to provoke discussion and further reading does apply in all these spheres.

It applies, too, in part-time adult teaching, as is carried out in WEA and extramural evening classes. Let us briefly compare this type of teaching with university teaching. The average age of the students attending evening classes is higher than of university students and the age-range is far wider (with the exception of the Open University), ranging upwards from 18–20 years of age into the sixties and even the seventies or higher. (I had one WEA student of eighty-two who did not miss a single class, handed in an essay a fortnight and presented me with some home-made mince-pies at the end of the Autumn term.) The students are usually of very mixed ability and experience but they are all highly motivated. They are paying for their course, giving up an evening a week regardless of fatigue or inclement weather, and they are frequently in full-time work – the exception being housewives, if this be considered part-time. They are not, in general, working for the attainment of a qualification.

The lecturer then is helped by the enthusiasm of the evening students: those who lack enthusiasm or discover that they dislike the subject matter or the teacher soon give up the course. On the other hand he has to maintain the interest of students who vary greatly in their capacity and who hope for entertainment as well as instruction. It is even more important in evening classes than in university lectures to provoke active discussion among the students. This involves picking a wary way between appearing overbearing or patronising on the one hand, and suffering voluble fools gladly, on the other. Since this book is concerned mainly with teaching in higher education it is perhaps worth pointing out that university teaching constitutes helpful preparation for the conduct of evening classes; and that the taking of evening classes is exceedingly helpful in teaching the inexperienced lecturer how to cope with university students. The differences between the two types of audience prove extraordinarily instructive.

Earlier in the chapter, I mentioned Colleges of Education: those institutions in which future school teachers are instructed in their art. It seems to me that many of the suggestions made in this book apply to those who train the young adults who will be the school masters and mistresses of tomorrow. Do the same desiderata hold in the actual teaching of children? In my view some, but not all, apply.

The term 'school-teaching' covers a very wide range – from pupils of five years or less to those of 17 or older. It is clear that the skills of interesting 'infants' and juniors differ from each other, and differ again from those needed in the middle and senior schools. Sixth-form teaching has many affinities with undergraduate teaching; at the other end of the scale, the 'infants' and juniors need quite a different approach. Let us therefore confine our attention to the middle age-range in school, that is pupils aged roughly 11 to 14, and compare the teaching requirements for them and for adult full-time students.

A major difference in the teaching conditions is that the schoolchildren's attendance at lessons is obligatory whereas that of the students at lectures is a matter of choice. A second difference is the fact, referred to in Chapter XIV, that students are drawn very much from the upper echelons of the nation's reserve of ability – about the top 15–20 per cent – whilst children in most schools, and in many classes, include the whole range of ability. Thirdly, the student is covering subject matter which is limited in scope and deliberately selected by him, whereas the middle school pupil is expected to take almost every subject that the school has to offer. A fourth difference, unlike in kind, is worth re-emphasizing: the school teacher has received instruction in how to teach and has had experience in so doing, as part of his training; the university teacher has had little or no such prior instruction and experience.

These differences carry certain implications for the teachers in schools and in universities. The first point to consider is the vexed question of discipline or class-control – 'first', because it is closely related to the first three of the above-mentioned points. Schoolchildren have usually been harder to manage, *en masse*, than adult students – though it must be admitted that, in recent years, both schools and universities present more disciplinary problems than in the past. Sporadic 'student unrest' apart, however, middle school children are harder to control than are young adults. Children are of course generally more vigorous and energetic than their elders and many of them have not yet learned to restrain the entirely normal aggressive impulses of the healthy young – especially the healthy young male. But other reasons probably contribute, notably that children's attendance at school is compulsory, that schools include a far higher proportion of unacademic pupils than do universities and that children have to go to many lessons whose subject matter holds no intrinsic interest for them.

The university teacher does not usually have disciplinary problems during lectures – not because he has the knack of controlling groups (he probably hasn't) – but because most of his dissatisfied customers chat quietly with their neighbours or doze or walk out rather than shout, let off stink-bombs, flick pellets or more seriously assault him. Nonetheless, a little training in managing unruly groups, as well as learning how to present his material and to pitch the level of difficulty, might prove useful to the potential lecturer, especially during the next decade or two.

Another difference, related perhaps to disciplinary problems, lies in the sanctions of school. The school teacher can, in theory, always invoke the aid of the head; and the head can, equally theoretically, invoke the aid of a child's parents – on such questions as truancy, bullying or insubordination. I say 'theoretically' because in practice the contemporary head and the contemporary parent sometimes abdicate responsibility. In any case, no such sanctions exist in higher education. The students have for the most part attained their majority when they come to university and if they choose to ignore the few remaining rules, these are often quite unenforceable.

Thus they are treated as adults in a way which was not true when the age of majority was 21 and when universities and colleges had a whole gamut of rules. It is difficult at this stage to say whether this change is desirable, partly because changes are rapidly taking place all the time. It may be argued that one becomes adult only by being treated as such; and that the earlier physical maturity of young people should be accompanied by earlier psychological maturity. On the other hand, it may be argued that the young need some framework against which to rebel and that it is frustrating to have nothing convincing to rebel against.

This leads to the still larger question of whether teachers – in school and in higher education – should instruct in accordance with a particular ideology or philosophy. Ought they to do so? If so, which one should they adopt? And should it be implicit in their teaching or explicitly stated? The frames of reference which have most frequently been used in this way, past and present, seem to be religion, Marxism/ Maoism, psychoanalysis and sociology. These resemble one another in that there is no way of proving or refuting them, that each contains a variety of sub-classes incompatible with one another, and that the upholders of each tend to say that their particular philosophy differs from the others in that it is fundamental and that its wholehearted acceptance is vital for the good of mankind. The proponent of each often takes the attitude that anybody who does not agree with him is blind or cowardly, a knave or a fool.

Religion is, perhaps, in a different category from the others in that for many years, in this country, it permeated education – just as Marxism does in the iron curtain countries and Maoism does in China. Recently in Britain, however, religion has loosened its hold, in both schools and universities, the religious not unnaturally claiming that the increasing violence, lawlessness and vandalism (and they are genuinely increasing) is due to the relaxation of religious standards. This confusion of religious theory with ethical conduct seems strange – in view of the many massacres and torturings committed in the name of one religion or another and the innumerable individuals who combine strongly felt religious principles with lives lacking in honesty and kindness towards others. These traits should I think be encouraged by educationists since communication is difficult in the absence of honesty, and life is bleak in the absence of kindness. But there is little evidence that Religious Education or Scripture effectively instil such virtues.

I would be in favour of teaching comparative religion in schools: this would serve the double purpose of instructing children about their cultural heritage, historical and literary, and of apprising them of the fact that one's religious beliefs and practices are largely a function of when and where one happens to be born. This is of interest to the anthropologically-minded and it might have the further merit of leading to religious toleration rather than the dogmatism which used to be inculcated.

The other ideologies, political and socio-psychological, should not I think be taught in schools – unless, perhaps, in the sixth form, again from a *comparative* viewpoint. They should certainly not be taught insidiously and by implication, under the guise of, for instance, 'history' or of 'economics', for this is indoctrination of the most disingenuous kind.

These problems do arise in higher education as well as in schools but the adult students tend to be more sophisticated intellectually and emotionally, and to have greater background knowledge against which to appraise what they are taught. If, moreover, the principles outlined above be followed by school teachers, future generations of university teachers may perhaps have acquired a better sense of proportion, a more critical approach to extreme ideologies and greater awareness of the dangers of subordinating ends to means.

The ends/means question is a suitable note on which to end. The main goals of education have been discussed in an earlier chapter. But we have not considered either the doctrine that the ends justify the means nor the fact that the means – when undesirable – contaminate the ends. Where the means are acceptable in themselves, the word 'contaminate' would hardly be appropriate but it is often the case that the type of means used strongly influences the end attained.

Those who adhere strongly to one particular ideology, especially if it be extreme, unshakeably believe that they *are right* and, therefore, that it is their duty to convert the world to their faith (unless and until they switch to another ideology, usually held with equal fervour).

They hold these beliefs so strongly that they believe also that the ends must be achieved, however violent, deceptive or ruthless the means. They should not be dismissed as 'wicked' – often they are genuine idealists – nor should they, in a democratic country, be gagged, imprisoned or exterminated for publicizing their views.

Thus we reach one of the great paradoxes. If tolerance and free speech and thought are among our educational goals, everybody – teacher and pupil; labourer, trade unionist and managing director; typist, housewife and bus conductress; the young, the old and the middle-aged – should be allowed to say and write what they wish. Yet, if the extremists take full advantage of this right, history and logic demonstrate that the right may thereby be lost. This is a paradox on which all teachers would do well to ponder. It underlies the whole fabric of education.

BIBLIOGRAPHY

1. ABERCROMBIE, M. L. J. (1966) 'Educating for change', *Universities Quarterly*, 21, 7–16.
2. BEARD, R. (1967) *Research into Teaching Methods in Higher Education*. London: SRHE.
3. BLIGH, D. A. (1972) *What's the Use of Lectures ?* Penguin Education.
4. CLARK, G. K. and CLARK, E. B. (1959) *The Art of Lecturing, some Practical Suggestions*. Cambridge: Heffer.
5. ENTWISTLE, N. J. and ENTWISTLE, D. (1970) 'The relationships between personality study methods and academic performance', *Brit. J. educ. Psychol.*, 40, 132–43.
6. EYSENCK, H. J. (1972) *Psychology is about People*. London: Allen Lane, The Penguin Press.
7. FURNEAUX, W. D. (1962) 'The psychologist and the university', *Universities Quarterly*, 17, 33–47.
8. HUDSON, L. (1960) 'Degree class and attainment in scientific research', *Brit. J. Psychol.*, 51, 67–73.
9. JONES, H. E. (1923) 'Experimental studies of college teaching', *Archives of Psychol.*, 68.
10. MALLESON, N. (1967) 'Medical students' study: time and place', *Brit. J. med. Educ.*, 1, 169–77.
11. McLEISH, J. (1968) *The Lecture Method*. Cambridge Institute of Education.
12. POWELL, L. S. (1973) *Lecturing*. Pitman.
13. QUILLER-COUCH, A. (1927) *A Lecture on Lectures*. London: Hogarth Press.
14. ROBINSON, E. (1968) *The New Polytechnic*. Penguin Education Special.
15. SHEFFIELD UNIVERSITY Academic Development Committee (1972). *Assessment of Students*. The University of Sheffield.
16. SMITHERS, A. (1970) 'What do students expect of lectures ?' *Universities Quarterly*, 24, 330–36.
17. TRENAMAN, J. (1951) The Length of a Talk. Unpublished paper (BBC Research Unit).
18. TROWN, A. (1970) 'Some evidence on the "interaction" between teaching strategy and personality', *Brit. J. educ. Psychol.*, 40, 209–11.
19. UNIVERSITY GRANTS COMMITTEE (1964) Report of the Committee on university teaching methods. Chairman: Sir E. Hale. London: HMSO.
20. WATT, I. (1964) 'The Seminar', *Universities Quarterly*, 18, 369–389.
21. WINNICOTT, D. W. (1974) *Playing and Reality*. Harmondsworth: Penguin Books.
22. WISPE, L. G. (1951) 'Evaluating section teaching methods in the introductory course', *J. educ. Res.*, 45, 161–186.

Longer bibliographies may be found in Bligh *op. cit.* and McLeish *op. cit.* The University of Newcastle-upon-Tyne has published a 42-page bibliography, entitled *University Teaching* (1974). This contains sections on Teaching Methods in specific disciplines, as well as general works, and contains also sections on

Evaluation, Group Teaching, Educational Psychology, Audio-visual Aids and Programmed Learning.

On the last two topics: (a) Liverpool University's Audio-visual Aids and Programmed Learning Unit have produced a 20-page pamphlet entitled *A Guide to Audio-visual Media* (1971). (b) British Universities Film Council have published a catalogue of *Audio-visual Materials for Higher Education* (1973).